From Micky V
to Greg # 70 -
B-day , 1/14/2017

The Church Under Attack

Diane Moczar

The Church Under Attack

Five Hundred Years That
Split the Church and
Scattered the Flock

SOPHIA INSTITUTE PRESS
Manchester, New Hampshire

Sophia Institute Press
Box 5284, Manchester, NH 03108
1-800-888-9344

www.SophiaInstitute.com

Sophia Institute Press® is a registered trademark of Sophia Institute.

Library of Congress Cataloging-in-Publication Data
Moczar, Diane.
  The church under attack : five hundred tears that split the church
  and scattered the flock / Diane Moczar.
    pages cm
  Includes bibliographical references.
  ISBN 978-1-933184-93-7 (pbk. : alk. paper) 1. Catholic Church—
  History—Modern period, 1500- 2. Church history—Modern
  period, 1500- I. Title.
  BX1304.M56 2013
  282.09'03—dc23

                                                      2013004100

First printing

Contents

Introduction

For anyone who studies the history of the West, particularly the history of the Church, the early period of that history, from the civilizations of Greece and Rome through the High Middle Ages, presents a marked contrast to the later period. Europe in the early period seems to progress from one cultural development to the next, as the Greek achievement is absorbed, preserved, and spread by Rome, as Christianity rises and flourishes, as the nations of Europe take shape and astonishing spiritual, intellectual, artistic, scientific, legal, governmental, and literary milestones are reached. Of course there are times of upheaval, war, and natural disaster, but the general course of civilization appears to be upward. For the Church in particular, progress is apparent in every area. It is true that the earliest Christian centuries saw the rise of formidable challenges to the Faith in the form of the great heresies such as Arianism, but those had been largely vanquished in the early centuries. Later sects came and went without seriously damaging the unity and harmony of Christendom. The creation of Catholic civilization throughout Europe, the development of Catholic social, economic, and political thought and institutions, the great masterpieces of Catholic art, architecture, philosophy, and literature are all features of that first period of European history.

With the sixteenth century, all this begins to change dramatically. The first of a series of great spiritual, intellectual, and cultural crises arises: the Reformation. It will be followed in subsequent centuries by other major assaults on Catholic belief and thought, assaults that have continued into our own time. It is the purpose of this book to trace the pattern of this later period of Western history, with particular emphasis on the state of the Church from the sixteenth to the mid-twentieth century, and to examine the major attacks on the Church in both early-modern and modern times. We must keep in mind, of course, that Catholic culture and the Western civilization that it formed did not dry up and blow away during the past few centuries. Great Catholic writers, scholars, scientists, rulers, and saints can be found in more recent times as well as in the distant past. It is true, as we shall find, that modern civilization on the whole has become deficient in many of the principles—moral, aesthetic, political, and spiritual—that lay at the heart of the Catholic civilization of the past, although the situation may not yet have reached the point of no return. Our task here is to examine how the events of the past few hundred years have shaped the present, both spiritually and temporally.

For each of the centuries discussed in this book, we will examine the major historical developments, including the wars, economic growth, achievements, and major cultural and political issues of concern to the people then living. We will especially focus on the condition of the Church in each period. Since it is people, and not impersonal forces, that make history, we will meet the kings, explorers, adventurers, villains, and saints of each period. Because our survey of modern history will necessarily be a cursory one—otherwise we would need several volumes for each century—many fascinating people and developments will receive briefer treatment than the reader might desire. This is why a few suggestions for further reading are included for each chapter, at the end of the book; they are by no means exhaustive treatments of the various topics, but most of them will lead the interested reader to a great many more works.

The Church Under Attack

Chapter 1

The Busy Sixteenth Century

The trouble with the sixteenth century is that the people living in it did far too much. Harried teachers faced with squeezing their doings into a tidy lecture would love to give them some advice: Stop doing things! Leave something for the next century! But no, the sixteenth-century populace wouldn't listen. Look to the west from Europe. There they go, beetling around Africa in their newfangled ships, getting seasick on the Atlantic routes to America, and staring openmouthed at the Pacific. Look east. There they are, warring with the Turks and winning battles too important for us to ignore. In India and the Americas they are planting colonies and creating empires, while fighting wars in Europe. And in northern Germany, a neurotic monk with a hammer in his hand and a couple of nails between his teeth is getting ready to tack a piece of paper to the door of a church. We won't be able to ignore him either. To make it worse, there were others who spent their part of the century scribbling plays with names such as *Macbeth* and *Othello* or novels such as *Don Quixote*. And the century was so chock-full of spectacular saints, heroes, and villains that, like its wars of religion, they spill over into the next century.

The Church Under Attack

We will deal first, in short, with the Reformation. Here I am using a conventional term, although the movement is more justly called the Protestant Revolution; some authors use *Protestant Reformation* and *Catholic Reformation*, but the more familiar terms seem to be *Protestant Reformation* and *Catholic Counter-Reformation*. I use the term *Reformation*, then, to mean the development, in the sixteenth century, of new religions organized in opposition to Catholicism. By the end of the century there would be dozens of new sects, but we will deal primarily with the three major ones: Lutheranism, Calvinism, and Anglicanism.

To start with poor Martin Luther, a psychologically complex monk with an intractable sense of guilt: we first find him — in 1517 — posting his famous ninety-five theses on the church door in Wittenberg, a traditional practice intended to signify that the hammerer wanted to open a debate on his ideas. If we asked Father Luther what he meant to accomplish, he would say, after he had spat out the nails and was in a position to answer us, that he wanted to publicize his criticisms of Catholicism and to make known the new doctrines he had been inventing for the last few years.

The myth about Martin Luther is that he was scandalized by the terrible corruption in the Catholic Church. He had been to Rome and saw the popes and cardinals living in luxury and vice, spending the money extracted from the faithful on pagan art to beautify Rome. He was shocked that the German clergy were not only depraved but teaching doctrines invented by the Roman popes that had little to do with "real" Christianity, and he wanted a return to apostolic purity of faith and morals. He was especially indignant about the new preaching of indulgences in Germany (the German states of the Holy Roman Empire):

people were encouraged to pay money in return for time off in purgatory for themselves or the release from purgatory of their deceased relatives.

Only one of these statements, the last, is strictly true. Pope Leo X wanted money to rebuild St. Peter's and apparently thought the way to get it was to send preachers around Europe to collect money in return for indulgences. In Germany, he had the support of an archbishop who needed to pay gambling debts and was given a share of the take. It was so obvious that this was an abuse that the Spanish hierarchy did not allow the indulgence hawkers into Spain.

The question is why so many people went along with the scam and parted with considerable cash in return for their time off in purgatory or that of their relatives. It seems to me that there are a number of reasons this abusive selling of spiritual favors was able to succeed to the extent it did. We are dealing here with a new business culture that had emerged late in the previous century, sometimes called proto-capitalism, in which money was plentiful but time was not. The busy merchants—like the one whose motto was "In the name of God and Profit"—were disinclined to spend time performing the works required to gain an indulgence. Recall, also, that loss of spiritual fervor of which many saints had complained during the later Middle Ages; after all, one must love God in order to pray, do penance, and cleanse one's heart with the goal of acquiring spiritual blessings, and that love of God, which St. Francis of Assisi had already seen fading in the thirteenth century, had now grown cold. Thus, when our spiritually tepid businessman heard that his time in purgatory could be reduced by paying a sum of money, he was all for it. The memory of those shady deals that had made him so successful bothered him sometimes, and he cared about ensuring a pleasant eternity for himself. When he realized that he could also discharge his neglected duties to the souls of his dear departed, he was even more eager to be in the first pew when the indulgence preacher began to speak.

Martin Luther was rightly indignant about this issue, but it was the occasion—not the cause—of his public proclamation of his novel theological ideas. For years before 1517 he had been a tormented monk and an unhappy priest, obsessed with guilt and developing startling new ideas on human nature and salvation. He was not simply indignant at the sinful lives of some clergy, nor was it even the spectacle of papal Rome during the Renaissance that scandalized him. He made use of these points later, but when he visited Rome as a younger man he seems to have said nothing about its moral failings. It was his new theology that absorbed him, and the indulgence issue gave him his opportunity to proclaim it.

A great deal could be said about Luther's ideas, his condemnation, and his role in German history, but we have room for only a few points here. Among the doctrines invented by Luther that were really new in Christian thought, five stand out as truly revolutionary. First, Luther saw human nature as totally depraved, although the Church had never taught this. Human nature is good because it is created by God, although because of Original Sin it has been weakened and beset by sinful tendencies. Secondly, because we are so depraved, thought Luther, we cannot help sinning. Indeed, everything we do—even "good" works—are sins: "Sin boldly, but believe more boldly still!" This amounts to a denial of free will. Thirdly, Luther distrusted reason: "Reason is the Devil's whore; it must be drowned at Baptism." This may echo the pessimism of William of Ockham, whose ideas were popular in sixteenth-century German universities. Again, it is opposed to the Catholic view of reason as the means by which we come to know truth, and therefore both good and necessary to faith. Fourthly, we come to the famous *sola fides* principle enunciated by Luther. Only faith, he declared, leads to salvation, and he defined *faith* subjectively, as a sort of "fiduciary trust" that Christ will save us. For the Catholic, faith is the assent of the intellect moved by the will and prompted by grace, to all the truths God has revealed. It is not of itself sufficient for salvation because we need hope, charity, and other virtues and "works" also. Lastly, *sola scriptura* was Luther's radical answer to the question of where the authentic teaching of Christ was to be found: in Scripture *alone*. Here he was rejecting the oral teaching of the Apostles transmitted by the Church (Tradition), as well as the dogmatic teachings of the popes and the councils. Any Christian who prayerfully reads Scripture, Luther thought, would be guided by the Holy Spirit to its meaning. No need for priests to explain what it meant.

As his new sect became organized, Luther decided it could do without priests, religious, most of the sacraments, and a hierarchy. When he realized there had to be some authority to settle disputes that might arise within the Lutheran community, he appealed to the local duke, saying that none of the community had received a calling to do the job, so would His Highness do it? His Highness was only too glad to do so; this was just what secular authorities in Germany had wanted all through the Middle Ages—the chance to control religion. Everywhere, in fact, the new Protestant religions would be imposed by lords and kings, and religion would become entangled with politics and an emerging nationalism. Carlton Hayes has written, "Protestantism is the religious aspect of nationalism"; Luther would announce, "I am the prophet of the Germans!" Within the Holy Roman Empire, dozens of princes, dukes, and other lords took sides for or against Luther based on political considerations, with many supporting him as a challenge to the young Catholic Emperor Charles V. Peasants took some of Luther's ideas so literally that they mounted a widespread revolt against their landlords, whereupon Luther urged merciless suppression of the "lying, thieving peasants," and tens of thousands were slaughtered. The empire threatened to disintegrate in religious upheaval and warfare, until Charles, horrified at the chaos and mindful of the massed armies of the Turks drawing ever nearer to his borders, came up with a solution. His Peace of Augsburg in 1555 stated that the religion of the prince was the religion of the people. Period. If your prince was Lutheran and you were Catholic, you could move, and vice versa. A non-solution if ever there was one, but at least it brought a temporary peace. The first new religion was now established.

The second new religion was made up by John Calvin, a Frenchman forced to flee France because of his heresies, who ended up setting up a Calvinist dictatorship in Geneva, Switzerland. Calvin took many of his ideas from Luther, but he was a more systematic thinker and produced the first compendium of Protestant theology. What Calvin is best known for is his extreme emphasis on predestination. From all eternity, he thought, God had destined some souls for heaven and some for hell, and nothing one could do would change the verdict. Calvin also implicitly denied free will, holding that man was so bad that he could will only evil: "Man is an ape, a wild and savage beast." Of course none of the inventors of the new religions proved their novel propositions or backed them up with miracles, but somehow they gained a following. Early Calvinists were often morbidly obsessed with the idea that they might be damned no matter what they did, but Calvin assured them that they could have signs that they were headed in the other direction. One sign was that they believed in Calvinism; another was good behavior. The surest sign, however, because it was the most objective, was that they would prosper in this world. It is only human to want assurance of salvation, and it is also human to make very sure that one has a visible guarantee of it by becoming a financial success. Businessmen were thus encouraged to become even more successful in their "godly" activity, while the stern Calvinist virtues of thrift, frugality, and sobriety promoted a culture of hard work. This development has led some historians to link Calvinism with the rise of modern capitalism, and certainly the promoters of capitalism and the work ethic were often Calvinists. As President Calvin Coolidge said, "He who builds a factory builds a temple; he who works there worships there."[1] This is the full-blown religion of work.

With their conviction that they were the righteous few destined for salvation and their suspicions about who the unsaved were (especially Catholics and the unsuccessful in general), the Calvinists became the radicals of the Reformation. In France they formed the political opposition to the Catholic kings and provoked decades of religious war; it was they too who desecrated Catholic churches in their hatred for the Blessed Sacrament they had so recently adored themselves, now profaned by them out of a fanatical horror of "idolatry." Their destruction of Catholic monuments, historic buildings, and art deprived the world of a priceless heritage. By the end of the sixteenth

---

[1] Calvin Coolidge, speech delivered to the Massachusetts senate in 1914: "Have Faith in Massachusetts."

century, the Calvinists had achieved toleration for their religion by the French government, and the second new religion was thus legitimized.

The third new religion came about by accident. Henry VIII of England was incensed because the pope would not give him a divorce from his wife so he could marry one of her ladies-in-waiting with whom he had become infatuated. Henry had no sympathy for Protestantism—he actually wrote a refutation of Luther's errors (unless his friend and chancellor, Thomas More, wrote it for him). When, however, he broke with the papacy over the divorce and made himself the head of the Church in England, the way was paved for all sorts of anti-Catholic ideas to infiltrate schismatic England and quickly take it into heresy. For political reasons, Henry's illegitimate daughter, Elizabeth, made England the champion of the Protestant cause in Europe, which turned out to be a highly successful move, as we shall see.

The consequences of the emergence of these three new sects were profound, and the effects of the Reformation continue to this day. But what of the Church? Was she really corrupt, and did she fight back when she was attacked on all sides? The answers are no and yes; as the next section will show.

Catholic Thought and Culture in the Sixteenth Century:
The Counter-Reformation

Catholic thought in the sixteenth century was dominated by the idea of reform long before Luther got going and even more so once the Reformation was in full swing. Once the Catholic Counter-Reformation moved into high gear in the latter half of the century, it triggered a spectacular cultural movement in which new forms of art, music, and literature were placed at the service of the Faith. While Protestantism, as Lord Kenneth

The Busy Sixteenth Century

Clark has remarked, did not create a new civilization or new artistic forms, Catholicism in the sixteenth and seventeenth centuries exploded in new styles of painting, architecture, sculpture, and music. The Baroque masterpieces are as lavish as the Calvinist churches were prim and plain; when captured Catholic churches became Puritan temples, their decorations were smashed and removed, and God no longer dwelled there. Baroque artists seemed eager to compensate for this barbarism (although sometimes they overdid it a bit) by creating magnificent settings for the Blessed Sacrament and an atmosphere of light, movement, and color within and without the Catholic churches that were built at the time. While Protestants were busy whitewashing priceless frescos in former Catholic churches, Baroque masters filled with beautiful artwork the walls and ceilings of numerous new Catholic churches.

Catholic writings of the period are among the classics of Western civilization: the mystical poetry of St. John of the Cross, the works of St. Teresa of Avila, including her engaging autobiography, St. Thomas More's *Utopia*, and St. Francis de Sales's *Introduction to the Devout Life* are only a few examples that reflect the energy of a revitalized Church. It now seems clear that Shakespeare was a closet Catholic living during the Elizabethan persecution in England (in which it seems that some of his relatives were hanged, drawn, and quartered), and certainly Catholic themes and veiled criticisms of tyranny occur in his plays.

How did it all get started? After all, the Church in the early sixteenth century, while not by any means mired in corruption, as the Protestants claimed, was certainly mired in one of her mediocre periods. Some of the popes acted more like the Renaissance princes they were than successors of Peter, and a few of them led lavishly immoral lives. As Professor Euan Cameron has recently shown, however, it is not true that all or even most monasteries were corrupt or that most priests were worldly (although it *is* true that ignorance was widespread among the clergy). Above all, Dr. Cameron's research found neither the widespread indignation against the Church that Protestants have claimed nor a desire among the people for any type of new religion. The Reformation got off the ground through a combination of political backing of the heresiarchs by local and national rulers and a cleverly orchestrated appeal to ordinary people to make up their own minds on dogma. For the first time, "doctrine was subjected to public debate,"[2] under the guidance of the Protestant leaders who formulated the terms of the debate — in the process distorting Catholic teaching and simplifying religious principles.

Thus the new sects, by the end of the sixteenth century, were proliferating wildly because, to Luther's dismay, the individual Protestant reading his Bible without an infallible guide drew his own conclusions and often went on to create his own little sect instead of agreeing with Dr. Luther. Each new group began to gather enthusiastic followers as well as political support. Where popular support was lacking, it could be enforced at gunpoint, and diehard Catholics could be permanently eliminated.

Meanwhile, the Fifth General Council of the Lateran had been called by Pope Julius II in 1512 to deal with various political quarrels with which he was concerned, both outside and within the Church. He died in 1513, and his successor, Leo X (Medici), continued the council for his own goals. It met only

---

[2] Euan Cameron, *The European Reformation* (Oxford: Clarendon Press, 1991), 422.

a dozen times, and while it made a few good rulings, it was by no means the spearhead of reform that it could have been. By an eerie coincidence, the sessions wound up in 1517, just a few months before Luther burst onto the religious scene. It took nearly thirty years for another council, the great Council of Trent, to take up at last the Protestant challenge and galvanize the movement for true Catholic reform. Trent met off and on from 1545 to 1563, correcting abuses the Protestants had protested and many more besides, and producing its great codification of Catholic doctrine, in particular the points challenged by the heresiarchs—justification and predestination, for example.

Even Trent could have remained a dead letter, had it not been followed by two of those divine surprises so frequently met with in Catholic history. First, a pope who was a saint, St. Pius V, came to the papal throne in 1566 and vigorously implemented the reforms mandated by Trent. (He had other tasks too, particularly the life-or-death struggle of Christendom with the Ottoman Turks, which we will see in another chapter.) Secondly, there suddenly appeared in the sixteenth and seventeenth centuries numerous highly gifted champions of the cause of the Church and of reform. Many of them are larger-than-life figures, both talented and saintly, and their number, holiness, and achievements are perhaps unprecedented in Catholic history. A number of them were Jesuits, of that Society of Jesus founded by an unlikely middle-aged soldier of fortune, Ignatius Loyola. Famous and heroic Jesuits included Francis Xavier, apostle of India and Japan; Francis Borgia—and who would have expected a saint from that sinister family?—Isaac Jogues and his companions, tortured to death for the entertainment of the American Indians to whom they had preached; St. Peter

Claver, "slave of the slaves," apostle of the African slaves in the South American slave port of Cartagena, and his colleague Father Sandoval, author of the first abolitionist tract; St. Claude de la Colombière, director of St. Margaret Mary Alacoque, risking his life in England during the persecution; and St. Edmund Campion and many other martyrs in England. This is only a partial list of the Jesuit saints of the Counter-Reformation period. Jesuits were zealous in promoting the reforming decrees of the Council of Trent, engaging in theological controversy, founding schools, carrying out papal diplomacy, and winning thousands of souls for Christ outside Europe to replace those lost to heresy in the Old World.

There were numerous non-Jesuit saints as well. In Spain, St. Teresa of Avila and St. John of the Cross founded the Carmelite reform, which spread throughout Europe, and wrote classics of mystical theology; St. Angela Merici was a pioneer in education for girls, and St. Jane de Chantal founded the Visitation Order in France under the direction of the great St. Francis de Sales. St. Vincent de Paul broke new ground in the organization of charity for the most needy and was also a great spiritual writer and director of souls. St. Philip Neri, through his unique Oratory, which attracted both clergy and laymen — among them great Italian scholars and artists — made Renaissance Rome once again a holy city.

This is only a short list of saints of the Counter-Reformation; I cannot include them all here. In fact, it would take volumes to give them their due and bring them to life — they were all extraordinarily vivid personalities with tremendous vitality and energy. We will meet still others in another context.

Despite the emergence of these champions, we must remember that Catholics in all the areas in which Protestantism was victorious suffered greatly for their faith, and in those areas—northern Germany, England, part of the Low Countries, and elsewhere—the millennial culture of Catholicism was badly disrupted, where it was not destroyed.

Eamon Duffy's prize-winning *Stripping of the Altars: Traditional Religion in England, 1400–1580* provides a harrowing evocation of what the change in religious practice meant to ordinary people. At one stroke, holy days, customs, prayers—including prayers for the dead—that had been part of people's lives and ways of thinking from time immemorial were abolished. There is an account of soldiers being sent into a village to enforce Protestant orthodoxy and snatching a rosary from the hands of an old woman at prayer. When the villagers attempted to defend her, the soldiers massacred them. In some places, depending on the monarch or the local authorities, practice swung back and forth between the old religion and the new sect, a development that caused its own peculiar spiritual damage. Then there was the sheer destruction of art objects and indeed anything smacking of Catholicism, particularly under "good" Queen Elizabeth. Michael Wood, BBC historian and documentary filmmaker, has compared the devastation to the tactics of the Taliban and the Chinese Cultural Revolution.

The results of the English gestapo's policies can perhaps be seen most clearly in the colonies founded by the Puritans in New England in the seventeenth century. It should be explained that the Church of England—the Anglican church—had kept some of the trappings of Catholicism. When, however, Calvinism began to filter into the country, with its determination to "purify" the official church of all Catholic elements, this "Puritanism" gradually became a force to be reckoned with.

The Church Under Attack

Originally shunned and penalized (which is why some of them went to America), the Puritans came to power in England by means of a revolution in the seventeenth century, as we will see. In America, however, they could give full scope to their bizarre ideas.

The following is a passage from a biography of the preacher Increase Mather, by Michael G. Hall. He first quotes another historian, Charles Hambrick-Stowe, on the goal of the Puritans: "The Puritan vanguard was dedicated to the destruction of an entire world view, a whole system of values and meaning woven from Roman liturgical forms and pagan religious traditions in their English manifestations. The clearest illustration of this 'purification' process was the Puritan renunciation of the ecclesiastical year according to saints' days and local agricultural legends." Professor Hall comments:

> The full thrust of this change in world view was not apparent until Puritans actually controlled the society in which they lived.... Once there [in America] and in control, the Puritans quickly and steadily replaced the traditional English village culture with a new one. Sports, dances, music, and games, whether practiced by the common villagers or gentle classes, all went.... Dress, adornment, and hair styles for both sexes, the upbringing of children, the conduct of business, there was nothing that was not reformed. Marriage became a civil service, no longer performed in church as a sacrament.[3] Not only saints' days, but "Christmas, Easter, and

---

[3] Michael G. Hall, *The Last American Puritan: The Life of Increase Mather* (Hanover, New Hampshire: Wesleyan University Press, 1988).

other high holy days disappeared from the calendar. For half a century, Boston shops and schools stayed open on December twenty-fifth. Even the names of months and days — either Roman or pagan in origin — were dropped, for antiseptic reasons. Monday, December 23 became 23d 10m. One small concession to tradition was to begin each year on March 25, Lady Day."

Space prevents a discussion of the Salem witch trials, which were another outgrowth of Puritanism.

We shall see that the same tactics — from regulating dress and other personal details to creating a new calendar — were used during the French Revolution, all with the goal of disrupting and abolishing the Catholic culture and mentality in France. Meanwhile in Puritan America, the right sort of literature had to be created also. Here are two brief excerpts from a book for children published in Boston as late as 1715: "Let thy Recreation be Lawful, Brief, and Seldom." "Let thy Meditations be of Death, Judgement, and Eternity." Where in this view is the loving Jesus who wanted the little children to come to Him?

It is a tonic for the soul to pass from this depressing atmosphere to the glorious exuberance of the Counter-Reformation, whether in the magnificence of the newly codified Mass; in the space and color of almost every baroque church, with its appealing paintings and sculptures, echoing with the hymns of Palestrina; or in the letters and books of the saints of the period — humane, humorous, and gentle, while filled with high spirituality. This is how the Church fought back. As Belloc famously put it, "Wherever the Catholic sun doth shine / There's always laughter and good red wine. / At least I've always found it so. / Benedicamus Domino!"

The Church Under Attack

The Sixteenth Century: Part II

While the Reformation was wreaking havoc throughout Europe, two other earthshaking events were in progress. Spain's conquest of the newly discovered Americas was proceeding with spectacular success, arousing the envy of Spain's bitter religious and political enemy, England. Meanwhile, gathering strength at the other end of the European continent was the greatest military threat that Christendom had ever faced: the assault on the West by the Ottoman Turks. Both these developments unfolded on a vast scale and had repercussions well beyond the sixteenth century. They are far too complex and important to deal with adequately in one chapter, but we can look at some of their features.

The Colonial Achievement of Spain

This first of our two oversize topics is directly connected with the second. The Ottoman Turks, mentioned above, were newcomers from the Asian steppes—converts to Islam—who had begun to encroach on the fringes of the Byzantine Empire in the fourteenth century. After conquering Greece, part of the Balkan Peninsula, and other Christian areas, they had taken Constantinople in 1453 and went on from strength to strength to create a formidable empire. Now, in the 1500s, they controlled all the sea routes from the West to the East. The Black Sea was a Turkish lake; the Persian Gulf was under the Turks' control, and they held the African coast from Egypt to Algeria.

This disruption of the ancient trade routes between Europe and Asia stimulated an intense search in the West for alternative ways to and from Asian markets. The rulers of rival nations, ambitious merchants, missionaries, and adventurers were all eager to overcome the Turkish blockade of travel to the East. New shipbuilding technology made long ocean voyages feasible for the first time, and new navigational devices made them safer. (It is probably unnecessary to mention here that no sixteenth-century person with even a rudimentary education believed the earth to be flat. I doubt if any educated person from ancient times on up had ever thought so, though I recall my own mother looking out on the horizon of the Pacific and remarking, "It sure looks flat to me.")

The Portuguese, encouraged by the enterprising Prince Henry the Navigator, were the first to explore the west coast of Africa and finally succeed in sailing around that huge continent to Asia. Because of the interest stimulated by Columbus's pioneering voyages, the Spanish went the other way: to what they soon realized were huge and unexplored land masses. Thus began the Spanish empire in the Americas. Its story would fill many volumes, but the conquest of Mexico will have to serve for one brief example.

The Aztecs, who had been ruling Mexico for over a hundred years at the time of the Spanish conquest, are among the most unpleasant people in history—possibly even outranking the ancient Assyrians, Canaanites, and Carthaginians. Like virtually all the Indian tribes of both South and North America, they practiced human sacrifice. With them, however, it was not a victim here and a victim there on high holy days, or occasional vengeance on a tribe they had been fighting. The whole of Aztec society, civilized, advanced, and refined as it was, was literally built upon the ritual murder of tens of thousands of victims each year. It was a matter of political policy as well as religious practice, apparently crafted by a sinister and extremely long-lived prime minister who used it as a means of controlling the many subservient tribes within the empire. It is particularly ghastly to realize how the loathsome practice affected all of Aztec society.

In *The Killing of History*, Keith Windschuttle quotes historian Inge Clendinnen's description:

> The killings were not remote top-of-the-pyramid affairs. If only high priests and rulers killed, they carried out most of their butchers' work *en plein air*, and not only in the main temple precinct, but in the neighbourhood temples and on the streets. The people were implicated in the care and preparation of the victims, their delivery to the place of death, and then in the elaborate processing of the bodies: the dismemberment and distribution of heads and limbs, flesh and blood and flayed skins. On high occasions warriors carrying gourds of human blood or wearing the dripping skins of their captives ran through the streets, to be ceremoniously welcomed into the dwellings; the flesh of their victims seethed in domestic cooking pots; human thighbones, scraped and dried, were set up in the courtyards of the households — and all this among a people notable for a precisely ordered polity, a grave formality of manner, and a developed regard for beauty.

It comes as no surprise to learn that when Cortez landed in Mexico in 1519 with about three hundred men, to attempt the conquest of perhaps fifteen million, he was joined by tens of thousands of Indians from tribes long victimized by the Aztecs. It was, in fact, they who made the conquest. The epic story of the Spaniards' arrival — their astonishment at finding a city far more sophisticated than those of their own country, their peaceful reception by the Emperor Montezuma, the series of accidents that caused fighting to break out when Cortez was absent from the capital, the strange death of the emperor at the hands of one of his own men—make for stirring reading. The battles were far more costly in Aztec lives than they needed to be because the Aztec warriors refused all incentives to surrender; they thought that if they were taken alive they would be gruesomely sacrificed, and so they fought grimly to the death.

What followed the conquest provides an interesting comparison with how the English (and the Americans later) treated Indians. Cortez rebuilt the Mexican capital, granting land to prominent Aztecs as well as his own men. Self-governing Aztec towns were set up, in which Spaniards had no right to live or work and in which the Indians used their native language. The only demands of the Spanish government were for taxes and the right of missionaries to preach. Conversions were not forced. Except for a small number of prisoners, Cortez allowed no slavery, and by 1534 he had established schools—including schools for Indian girls—and the first hospital for Indians. The first printing press in the New World was set up in 1539, turning out translated material for the Indians; orphanages, trade schools, colleges, and even—a most ambitious undertaking—a university for Indian students.

No one pretends that there were no abuses of Indians by some of the conquerors (and vice versa, of course), but they were recognized as abuses and condemned. To curb the cruelty of some of Cortez's successors, the king of Spain appointed the bishop of Mexico "protector of the Indians"—and the first of these protectors managed to get an abusive governor removed. While the pope, in 1537, excommunicated those who enslaved or robbed Indians, King Philip III abolished all Indian servitude and the employment of Indians on sugar plantations by the end of the century. In spite of these measures, many of the Aztecs remained disaffected from Christianity because of ill treatment by some conquistadors; the missionary efforts of the zealous and humane Franciscans seemed to make little progress. It was then that our Lady intervened with the spectacular series of apparitions, in 1531, by which she became known as Our Lady of Guadalupe, Patroness of the Americas.

When the miraculous image of our Lady—one of those mysteries that scientists are at a loss to explain—appeared on the cloak of an Aztec Indian, St. Juan Diego, it immediately became a magnet for the native peoples of Mexico, drawing them to Christ. The symbolism of the image, the miracles connected with it, and the grace that flowed from it resulted in the mass conversion of the Indians—approximately eight million souls within about six years.

The fact that conquered and conqueror now shared the true religion encouraged intermarriage between the two races and the development of a homogeneous society. In a later century, a descendant of the Aztec emperor Montezuma was actually appointed to the highest political position in Mexico and ruled as Viceroy. (It was, as one historian has remarked, as if a great-grandson of Sitting Bull had become president of the United States.) A comparison of the Spanish record in the New World with that of the English and the Americans, as far as treatment of the Indians goes, is almost laughable. Where were the English colonial hospitals, orphanages, and schools for the Indians? It is interesting to note that when the smallpox vaccine was developed, the Spanish king immediately had it sent to the New World to be used for the Indians. During one of the many conflicts of the British with the Indians, however, the English sent their enemies a "present" of blankets—inoculated with smallpox bacillus.

The Wars with the Ottoman Turks

It was, of course, the Faith that made all the difference in the way the Catholic Spanish and the Protestant English behaved in the New World. The two nations were the great rivals of the sixteenth century, particularly during the second half, when Elizabeth of England had espoused the Protestant cause everywhere and Philip II of Spain was the Catholic champion of Europe. The enmity between heresy and truth colored their diplomatic, political, economic, and colonial struggles.

Bitter as it was, however, the many-faceted struggle waged by Spain against her greatest European rival almost paled beside the even more formidable danger that threatened the very existence of Christendom: the Ottoman Turks. The Turks were not a gang of enterprising merchants out to monopolize the major trade routes and make a lot of money. They were a disciplined, often brilliantly led and redoubtable nation of warriors out to conquer the world for Islam. Under Suleiman II, called the Magnificent for his patronage of culture, as well as the beautiful buildings with which he adorned his capital, the Ottoman Empire was at the pinnacle of its strength. Suleiman came to the throne in 1520 and declared war on Hungary the following year—on the pretext that the Hungarian king had not congratulated him on his accession.

During the previous century, the Turks had attempted to take the then-Hungarian fortress of Belgrade and been repelled by a legendary defense led by the great Hungarian leader Janos Hunyadi and the Italian preacher St. John Capistrano. In Albania too the Ottomans had been held off by the great hero known to history and legend as Skanderbeg. Since then, both Belgrade and Albania had fallen, and Suleiman was eager to follow up the Turkish successes. It became clear that the conquest of Hungary would be only the first step toward the conquest of the European continent; once it fell, the road through Vienna and thence to the heart of Europe would be open. Suleiman took a leisurely five years to build up an army of seventy to eighty thousand regular troops, with perhaps forty thousand irregulars.

Meanwhile, the Hungarians appealed for help to the nations of Christendom, but the young Holy Roman Emperor Charles was preoccupied with the Lutheran revolt and the chaos of the Peasants' War, and the Hungarian King Lajos faced the Turkish onslaught with an army that was outnumbered more than four to one. He died in the desperate retreat, and the Turks occupied most of the ancient country of Hungary for two centuries. Suleiman made two attempts on Vienna in 1529 and 1532, but both times he arrived too late in the year and ended up withdrawing. Before he got around to another try, he died in 1566 while besieging a stubborn Hungarian castle. He left his son, Selim II, "the Drunkard," a grim character lacking in the chivalrous qualities of his father, an empire of forty thousand square miles and an undefeated fleet. Selim would count on that fleet for his own assault on the West. Providentially, St. Pius V—who would become Selim's nemesis—had been elected pope the year before the accession of the new emperor.

Selim's plan was to attack on a number of fronts. The Turkish fleet would turn the Mediterranean into a Muslim lake, occupying the numerous islands and raiding the coasts of Italy, France, and Spain (perhaps they wouldn't even need to attack France, since it was frequently allied with the Ottomans at this time). Meanwhile those Moors whom Ferdinand and Isabella had expelled from Spain would invade the country from North Africa, counting on the support of the Moors who had remained there. If these measures succeeded, it would become a simple matter to mount a massive attack on Vienna, thus striking Europe from the east, west, and south. They very nearly succeeded.

Pope St. Pius realized the danger when the Ottoman fleet began its campaigns in the eastern Mediterranean in the 1560s and tried in vain to call a crusade. In his great poem *Lepanto*, Chesterton describes the results of the summons: "The cold queen of England [Elizabeth] is looking in the glass;/The shadow of the Valois [wishy-washy French king] is yawning at the Mass;/From evening isles fantastical rings faint the Spanish gun [the Spanish are busy in the Americas]..." When a Christian fleet was finally assembled in Italy, it included ships only from Spain—led not by King Philip II but by his illegitimate young half-brother, Don Juan—from the Papal States, from Venice, and from a few other Italian states. The formidable Knights of Malta were also there. This alliance was known as the Holy League. The total of 208 vessels was considerably less than the Turks' approximately 288, but the Christians had one great advantage: our Lady sailed with them. Not only had the pope called on all Catholics to pray the Rosary for victory, but the flagship of the Genoese Admiral Doria bore a picture of Our Lady of Guadalupe that had been touched to the original image in Mexico.

The story of the Battle of Lepanto on October 7, 1571, one of the great naval battles of history, has often been told. Suffice it to say here that it was a spectacular victory for the Holy League and put an end to major Turkish offensives against Europe by sea. Selim's grand plan to add Europe to the empire of the sultans had failed, but we will meet the Turks again at the massive second siege of Vienna in the following century.

Chapter 2

The Seventeenth Century

If the seventeenth century seems, at first glance, somewhat less cluttered than the sixteenth, it is only because the major events in Europe and North America tend to fall into three main categories: the ongoing struggle of Protestants against Catholics, the campaigns against the Ottoman Turks, and an intellectual movement of vast importance: the Scientific Revolution.

We will start by examining the depressing seventeenth-century consequences of the sixteenth-century religious revolution. These include a revolution in England of a kind heretofore unheard of in Christendom, in which a legitimate king was violently replaced by a fanatical dictator, and the near genocide of Irish Catholics along with the destruction of their country; later we will take up the first great European war—an eerie dress rehearsal for World War I—that involved most of the continent and brought untold suffering and death to Europe.

We will encounter some genuinely noble and heroic characters, some of them saints, and not all of them doomed to gruesome death at the hands of Calvinists. We'll watch one of the great battles of history, as the Turks are routed from their massive attack on Vienna and a very young and great general defeats them again and again until, by the end of the century, much of the Christian territory conquered by the Turks centuries earlier has been liberated.

In this section, then, we'll start with the situation in England. When, at long last, Queen Elizabeth died, her successor was—ironically—the son of her archrival, the Catholic Mary Queen of Scots, whom Elizabeth had executed. Catholics had suffered so much under Good Queen Bess that they greeted James I with great optimism; they knew he had been raised a Protestant, but just possibly some of his mother's religion had rubbed off on him, or at least he might be inclined to tolerate it. They were soon disappointed. Pompous James with his Scots accent does not seem to have been really popular with anybody, although he did have the first permanent English settlement in America, Jamestown, founded in 1607, named after him. The only thing that saved Jamestown from disaster in its early years was the decision to cultivate, market, and promote tobacco. James disliked tobacco and called it "a noxious weed"; had he used his royal power to suppress the stuff, he might have saved the world from lung cancer.

James had trouble with Parliament, which considered him extravagant, and for a while after his arrival in England, it looked as if he was not going to enforce the laws forbidding all but the Anglican religion. He soon began to do so, however, going so far as to require even the Irish to attend Anglican services, contrary to an earlier treaty. By 1605 his measures against the Catholics appear to have led a few of the more unbalanced among them to plot his demise. They planned to blow up the parliament building on a day when James would be there, thus neatly disposing of most of the persecuting government, but the plot was discovered before it could be carried out. The

The Seventeenth Century

Gunpowder Plot remains murky and controversial; it seems to have had no chance of succeeding and certainly had nothing to do with the many innocent Catholics who were rounded up, tortured, and executed. This crackdown on dissidents was also the reason for the Calvinist immigration to New England in 1620, mentioned in the preceding chapter.

James was succeeded by his son Charles I, a more religious and dignified man who was married to a Catholic and thus did not make a very good persecutor. He was disinclined to enforce the religious laws and even permitted the Irish to practice their Faith in private. His patronage of George Calvert, a Catholic convert, included granting him a piece of land in America (the future Maryland) along with a charter allowing Catholics to settle there. By mid-century, Calvinists of various stripes largely controlled the English Parliament and increasingly opposed the king on everything from finance to religion. On their principle of private interpretation, they used texts from the new King James Bible to justify their increasingly radical agenda, finding support in Scripture for regicide, revolution, civil war, and much else. As Auguste Comte observed, "All revolutionary ideas are only social applications of the principle of private interpretation."

We cannot follow the ins and outs of Charles's dissolving and then recalling Parliament, or the various crises of his reign. Once the Puritans gained control of Parliament, their immediate goals were to control the entire government and to impeach the queen. This led to the English Civil War of 1642 to 1648 between the Puritans, led by Oliver Cromwell, and forces loyal to the king. It ended with the defeat of the king and the emergence of a more radical agenda: the Puritans now wanted not merely a submissive king, but no king at all. In one of the most dramatic trials in history, Charles was sentenced to death as a "tyrant, traitor, murderer, public enemy"—none of which he was. "How," he asked, "can any free-born citizen of England call life or anything else he possesses his own, if power without right daily destroy the old fundamental laws of the land? I speak not for my own right alone but also for the true liberty of all my subjects, which consists not in the power of government, but in living under such laws and such a government as may give the people the best assurance of their lives and property." On January 30, 1649, Charles I went bravely to his death. He asked for an extra shirt so he would not shiver from the cold and be thought a coward. "I am going from a corruptible to an incorruptible crown," he said, "where no disturbance can be." As he gave a memento to the bishop standing nearby he said, "Remember"—a future watchword of the Stuart cause.

Now began the bizarre reign of Oliver Cromwell, far more of a tyrant than King Charles ever was. The few non-Puritan members of Parliament were evicted, and the remaining few dozen supported Cromwell, who insisted that he held his "calling" from God. England was divided into military districts, and Puritan standards were enforced: Christmas was abolished, theaters closed, and other elements of English life frowned on by the "Saints" were eliminated.

Meanwhile, Charles's dashing young son, the future Charles II, was leading the resistance to Cromwell, sometimes in England (where he traveled in disguise and had hair-raising adventures), sometimes from abroad. The Irish rising in favor of Charles II in 1649 brought down the infamous invasion by Cromwell that has forever blackened his character, even in the eyes of those who find good things to say about him otherwise. As Antonia Fraser puts it, he lost control of himself and gave vent to his "total hatred for a way of life." At the siege of Drogheda, thousands were butchered when Cromwell flew into one of his famous rages and turned the city over to his troops for "a day and a night of uncalculated butchery." Besides the three thousand dead, some fifty thousand were sold into slavery in the West Indies. Even when his rage subsided, Cromwell apparently did not repent of the atrocity; indeed, he called it "a righteous judgment of God upon these barbarous wretches." Similar scenes were repeated in other Irish cities. Irish farms were confiscated and the dispossessed owners driven onto barren and unproductive land.

Charles II had also been in Scotland, where he was crowned, so it was then Scotland's turn to feel Cromwell's wrath. Here he was more conciliatory, killing only a few thousand. Back home, he found Parliament insufficiently docile, so he flew into another rage, threw the symbols of its authority on the floor, and declared it dissolved. At length, and probably to everybody's relief, he died in 1658 of—surprisingly, considering how many people had reason to hate him—natural causes. He was briefly succeeded by his son, but people were tired of the Puritan dictatorship and more than ready to welcome the Restoration, when Charles II came triumphantly to the throne of his ancestors.

Thus Oliver Cromwell, in my view, is a monster if ever there was one, although he is much praised in history books. There is an apt passage in a book by a Soviet defector on the workings of Russian intelligence. The author, writing under the pseudonym Suvarov, comments: "Millions are killed only by those who consider themselves good.... The most monstrous crimes in the history of mankind were committed by people who did not drink vodka, did not smoke, were not unfaithful to their wives, and fed squirrels from the palms of their hands." A neat description of Oliver Cromwell, who certainly didn't drink vodka. (I don't know about his relations with squirrels.) Only one pathetic scene causes me to look with something like pity on the butcher of Drogheda, and it occurred on his deathbed. A Puritan elder of some kind was sitting at his bedside and Cromwell asked, "Is it possible to fall from grace?" The minister replied, "No, it is not." "I am glad," Cromwell said, "because I know I was in grace once." The stark horror of this dialogue chills the reader. The dying man is looking back over his life and finds at least something that makes him think he has fallen from "grace." What he needs most desperately, of course, is sacramental confession. Instead, he gets the appalling statement that he could not possibly have fallen: once saved, always saved. He was predestined, according to Calvinist thinking, no matter how many atrocities he committed. And thus he passed into eternity. Surely we can pity him, at least in those final moments.

Charles II had his troubles with Parliament too but managed to die a natural death, becoming a Catholic on his deathbed. Since he had no legitimate heirs, it was agreed that his middle-age Catholic brother, James, a widower, would succeed him, provided that James's daughters were raised Protestant. Thus the anti-Catholics were assured of an annoying but probably short reign by a hated Catholic, made tolerable by the prospect of returning to a cozy Protestant succession under his daughters. But just when they were feeling good about this, history had a surprise for them. James married a young French Catholic, and before the anti-Catholics knew where they were, little James III, a baptized Catholic and heir to the throne, was wailing in his cradle. Immediately rumors were spread of a "substituted child," supposedly dug up somewhere by the duplicitous Catholics to ensure their hold on power. Possibly no one really believed this, even at the time, but all the Protestants agreed that something had to be done to prevent the perfectly legal succession of James's little son.

Over in Holland, William of Orange, husband of Mary, one of the Protestant daughters of James II, wrote a letter of congratulation to his father-in-law on the birth of his son. Simultaneously he ordered mobilization for the invasion of England to enforce his wife's claim to the throne. In England, James's other Protestant daughter, Anne, deserted her father to join the sedition. When the invasion came, James found himself also deserted by his own general (Churchill) and too short on loyal troops to make a successful resistance. He had already sent his wife and son to France and now prepared to follow them. The nearly victorious Protestants were willing to let him go (they were not keen on decapitating yet another king), but the word had not reached a keen-eyed fisherman on the riverbank who spotted the fleeing monarch and took him prisoner, thinking to please the traitors now in power. Instead, he placed them in the awkward position of having to let James escape again, this time with no embarrassing slip-ups. All this, if you can believe it, is called the Glorious Revolution (1688).

William and Mary, now reigning gloriously, issued the famous English Declaration of Rights in 1689, granting various rights to their subjects, although not, of course, to *all* their subjects. Hence provisions such as this one: "That the subjects which are Protestants may have arms for their defense suitable to their conditions and as allowed by law." If you're not a Protestant, forget the arms for defense. The declaration also, in effect, reduced the power of the king in favor of Parliament, to which William owed his crown. The triumph of Protestantism in England was reinforced by anti-Catholic laws forbidding

Catholics to inherit land, become priests, hear Mass, or send their children abroad for Catholic schooling. The last gasp of serious Catholic resistance was the brief War of the English Succession in 1689–1690. James II rallied support in Ireland, which William promptly invaded with his army, defeating the Irish at the Battle of the Boyne in 1690 while James fled again to France. By the Treaty of Limerick in 1691, William offered the Irish general Sarsfield various religious and civil rights for Irish Catholics, but the terms were almost immediately violated by the English and the infamous Penal Laws subsequently enacted. A million acres of Irish land were confiscated, and the owners reduced to beggars; clergy were to leave the country on pain of hanging, drawing, and quartering. The Irish were forbidden to vote, buy land, receive an education, or attend Catholic worship. The laws stopped just short of forbidding them to breathe.

In the Catholic colony of Maryland, the Glorious Revolution was a catastrophe. The colony had flourished, despite antagonism and sometimes armed invasion from Virginia. Indians were protected and many were converted by Jesuit missionaries; there was intermarriage between Indians and settlers. In 1641 the first black man in the colony, a former indentured servant, was elected to the Maryland General Assembly. Following the Revolution, however, the Church of England became the established church in Maryland. Catholics were denied civil rights, the Mass was illegal, and execution was the punishment for making converts. One measure, which sounds more like Stalinist law than anything else, provided that a Catholic child who apostatized had a right to all his parents' possessions.

Thus the seventeenth century was catastrophic for the Faith in England, America, and Ireland, and the Irish especially would continue to suffer extreme hardship and persecution for another two centuries. Irish humor, which no laws could suppress, mocked the situation. A sign posted by the authorities on the walls of Brandon supposedly read: "Enter here, Turk, Jew or atheist; any man except a papist." Underneath an Irishman had scrawled, "The man who wrote this wrote it well, for the same is writ on the gates of Hell."

Seventeenth Century II: Europe

When we leave Protestant England for the continent of Europe, we once more breathe Catholic air—if we are careful to steer for France, that is, and not the Holland that gave us William of Orange. After the many and varied characters we saw popping up throughout the history of seventeenth-century England, it is a relief to find a somewhat simpler political situation in France during the same period. The good news is that seventeenth-century France has only two kings. The bad news is that they are both named Louis (we can tell them apart by their last names, which are Roman numerals: Louis XIII and Louis XIV).

This period, in fact, begins the political ascendancy of France and is also in many ways the golden age of French culture and spirituality, which we will explore in a later section. To go with the two kings, who began their reigns as minors, we find two queen mothers and two great prime ministers who were cardinals. Here we will meet Louis XIII, who began his reign under the regency of his Italian mother, Marie de Medici. As a foreigner, she was less than popular with the French and tended to rely on an ambitious cleric named Richelieu, whom she assisted in becoming both cardinal and chief minister. So powerful and competent was he that he was sometimes said to be the true ruler of the country. His twin goals were to make the monarch all powerful in France, and France all powerful in Europe. To achieve the first goal, he had to destroy the independence of the powerful French Calvinists, who were known as Huguenots. As a result of the religious settlement of the wars of religion that had raged between Protestants and Catholics during the previous century, the Huguenots had been given much more than toleration. They maintained private armies, controlled a number of walled towns, and felt strong enough to revolt against the government — with English help — in 1625. Cardinal Richelieu was determined to break Huguenot power — not out of any particular devotion to the Catholic religion, but because Huguenot power stood in the way of his own and the king's absolute control of the country.

Young King Louis, on the other hand, known to his subjects as "the Just," cared about the spiritual dimensions of the crisis. St. Louis de Monfort wrote in his *Secret of the Rosary*:

When King Louis the Just, of blessed memory, was besieging La Rochelle, where the rebellious heretics had their strongholds, he wrote to his mother to beg her to have public prayers offered for a victorious outcome. The Queen Mother decided to have the Rosary recited publicly in Paris in the Dominican church of Faubourg Saint-Honoré, and this was carried out by the Archbishop of Paris. It was begun on May 20th, 1628.

Both the Queen and the Queen Mother were present, with the duke of Orleans, Cardinal de la Rochefoucauld, Cardinal de Berulle, and several other prelates. The court turned out in full force as well as a great number of the general populace. The Archbishop read the meditations on the mysteries aloud and then began the

The Seventeenth Century

Our Father and Hail Mary of each decade, while the congregation of religious and lay-folk answered. At the end of the Rosary a statue of the Blessed Virgin was carried solemnly in procession while the Litany of our Lady was sung.

This devotion was continued every Saturday with admirable fervor and resulted in a manifest blessing from heaven, for the King triumphed over the English ... and made his triumphant entry into La Rochelle on All Saints' Day of the same year. This shows us the power of public prayer.

After the victory in 1629, Richelieu bequeathed the Protestants religious toleration and the right to hold public office; only their fortifications were destroyed. This settlement would become an issue during the following reign. Like most early modern kings and ministers, Richelieu streamlined the French government and created an efficient bureaucracy, still with the goal of getting control over a country almost hopelessly attached to local customs, rights, and ways of managing business and politics without the central government's interference. Here he was only partly successful, but he did succeed in increasing revenue and strengthening the king's authority.

Much more controversial were some of the means taken by the cardinal to increase French power in Europe, particularly his manipulation of the brutal Thirty Years' War in the neighboring Holy Roman Empire. Here we might as well turn our gaze temporarily from seventeenth-century France to its imperial neighbor on the east. (The reader should consult a map here, for an idea of just what this sprawling territory in the heart of Europe included.) The heartland of the empire was its collection of hundreds of German states, each with its own tradition and way of doing things; we recall that Martin Luther started the Reformation in the northeastern German state of Saxony. Besides Germans, the empire in the early seventeenth century included Flemings, Dutch, Slavs, French, Italians, and a sprinkling of Danes and other ethnic groups. While most of the empire was Catholic, as were the Hapsburgs who ruled it, the Reformation had left its mark. For those princes who chafed at Hapsburg rule and wanted more independence and political power, Protestantism became a weapon to be used against the emperor.

It may be recalled that the Peace of Augsburg had imposed a makeshift curb on religious turmoil with the empire by stipulating that the religion of the prince was to be the religion of the people: move or convert, in other words. At the time, the only two religions in question were Catholicism and Lutheranism; by 1618, there was another, and far more radical, religious community within the empire: the Calvinists. There was no place for them in the Augsburg settlement, and their dissatisfaction grew. Other friction developed over other stipulations of the Peace of Augsburg, such as those concerning the restitution of property seized by Lutherans from Catholics. There was even Lutheran-Calvinist hostility.

In this unstable religious and political atmosphere, a local crisis developed in Bohemia. From here on, some readers may be reminded of a modern parallel in the progression from local blowup to devastating international conflict: the Thirty Years' War sometimes appears as a chilling preview of World War I. The Hapsburg Emperor Matthias had been elected King of Bohemia by the ruling elites, both Protestant and Catholic. He then appointed a council of regents whose policies

were unpopular in largely Calvinist Bohemia, and the Bohemians protested unsuccessfully to the emperor. In 1618, the
disgruntled Bohemian representatives marched to the building
where the regents met and resorted to what seems to have been
a Bohemian practice that occurs more than once in their history: defenestration. As its Latin root implies, this word means
"throwing out the window," which is what happened to the
hapless and terrified regents. (If you take a tour of Prague, you
can still see the window.)

I cannot resist quoting a little essay one of my students
found on the Internet, discussing the usefulness of the practice.
The victim "need not be a head of state, it could be a manager,
a spouse, even a much-too-elderly relative ... junior misbehav-
ing at bath time? Why not throw the baby out with the bath
water?" The article stressed the convenience, ease, speed, and
low cost of the method and wound up, "When there's just no
time for decapitation, you can always count on defenestration."
So the Bohemians thought. Fortunately for the royal officials,
they came to rest in either a garbage pile, a manure heap, or a
moat—depending on which account of the incident one ac-
cepts—from which they were able to scramble to safety.

The Bohemians then set up their own government and in
1619 elected as king a Calvinist from a neighboring territory,
Prince Frederick of the Palatinate, instead of Matthias's successor, the new Emperor Ferdinand. This was awkward for Frederick, because, as one of the electors of the empire, he had just
voted for Ferdinand, whom he was now supposed to replace on
the throne of Bohemia. His embarrassment did not stop him
from accepting the job, however, especially as his father-in-law,
James I of England, was supporting his cause. All over Europe,
in fact, Protestant rulers began to stir and consider what they

could get out of fighting the Hapsburgs. Thus what could have been a purely local conflict between the emperor and a rebellious state within his empire grew by stages into a conflagration that involved most of the states of Western Europe.

Briefly, the stages of the war were four:

- The period from 1618 to 1625 is known as the Bohemian Phase, in which imperial troops fought the Bohemian rebels and won. The war could have ended at that point, but then came

- the Danish Phase, 1625–1629. The Danes decided to intervene, both to help their fellow Protestants and to occupy imperial territory that had been in dispute between the empire and Denmark. Meanwhile, the Spanish Hapsburgs, relatives of the emperor, had begun sending him aid; Protestant Dutch pirates captured the Spanish treasure fleet, but the phase still ended with victory for the Catholic forces. However,

- the Swedish Phase, 1630–1635, was initiated by Cardinal Richelieu. Contrary to what might reasonably be expected of a Catholic cardinal, he bribed Swedish King Gustavus Adolphus, a Protestant, to take Sweden into the war against the Catholic empire—for purely political reasons. He wanted to weaken all rivals to the ascendancy of France. Spanish soldiers were now joining the imperial troops, as international involvement spread. (It should also be noted that all this havoc occurred within the Empire, mostly in increasingly devastated German areas.) Despite the military innovations and battlefield tactics developed by King Gustavus, the Protestants lost this phase too. Gustavus was unexpectedly killed, and although the Swedes rallied, they were unable to prevent a Catholic victory. This time both sides had had enough, and they drew up a peace treaty. But

- the longest and most destructive phase—the French or International Phase, 1635–1648—was still ahead of them, because Richelieu would not allow peace to break out. He declared war on Hapsburg Spain and sent troops into the German states of the empire to keep the chaos going, in the political interests of France. A student once asked me why the pope did not do something about Richelieu. Urban VIII did try repeatedly to persuade the cardinal that his policies were bringing suffering and destruction to countless victims of his inordinate ambition. He strongly urged him to stop promoting the most horrible war Europe had ever seen, but Richelieu was not among those who pay attention to popes. It took the divine Superior of all popes, emperors, and even cardinals to remove Richelieu from the scene, through his death in 1642. Emperor Ferdinand and Prince Frederick had already died, and Louis XIII was to die the year after his Machiavellian minister.

The way was finally clear for the restoration of peace by the Treaty of Westphalia in 1648. By the terms of this treaty, Calvinists were admitted to the Augsburg settlement, thereby acquiring religious rights within the empire. The major protagonists were to hold on to the territories they had occupied, which benefited Sweden, France, and various German states that had joined the revolt against the emperor. Some of the major results of this deadly international conflict were the following:

- The Holy Roman Empire as an international organism began to give way to nation-states; the more than three hundred states the empire comprised became virtually autonomous, to the point of conducting their own foreign policy.

- The Hapsburgs, weakened as emperors, began to consolidate their strength in their hereditary lands in central and eastern Europe.

- War had become much more deadly and destructive due to developments in weaponry and tactics made in the course of this war.

- The German states were so completely devastated that some areas lost two-thirds of their population and five-sixths of their villages.

- Christendom was now permanently split, facing a future of aroused nationalism and near-constant war — no longer motivated by religion but by worldly goals such as power, money, prestige, and natural resources.

- France had become the most powerful nation in Europe; Richelieu had won all right, although whether that gratified him in his new abode the historian cannot say. As the pope said, on hearing of the cardinal's death, "If there be a God, the Cardinal de Richelieu will have much to answer for. If there be none, why, he lived a successful life."

The Seventeenth Century

This first half of the century on the continent of Europe was thus dominated by some of the worst consequences of the Reformation, including revolt against lawful authority on religious pretexts and the confusion of religious and political interests we have already seen emerge during the Reformation itself. There is much more to this many-sided period, however, both in the intellectual and cultural realms and, in the final two decades of the century, in the spectacular campaigns that expelled the Ottoman Turkish armies from much of the European territory they had conquered and so tenaciously held since the fourteenth and fifteenth centuries. These will be the subjects of the next section.

The Seventeenth Century III:
Expelling the Turks from Europe

The Ottoman Turks had been nibbling at the fringes of eastern and southern Europe since the fourteenth century, sometimes being repulsed, but always returning to the attack and finally boldly conquering one Christian state after another. In the sixteenth century we were heartened by the unlikely victory of an outnumbered Christian fleet against the great Ottoman navy at Lepanto in 1571. That spectacular Turkish defeat neutralized a brilliant Ottoman plan to secure control of the entire Mediterranean, attack the coasts of southern Europe by sea, and assist the Moors of North Africa—expelled from Spain in 1492—to reinvade and reoccupy the Iberian Peninsula. We recall also that one Turkish attempt against Vienna had been made by the great Suleiman the Magnificent in 1529, but he had deemed it prudent to withdraw after gauging the probable costs of taking the city and realizing that it was too late in the year to start a major siege.

The Church Under Attack

Now, near the end of the seventeenth century, another great Turkish campaign was about to be launched, "the most important campaign in Turkish history," according to *The New Cambridge Modern History*. It involved a Turkish army of perhaps half a million men, with the goal of consolidating Ottoman rule over areas that had been incompletely subdued—Hungary especially, where regions and individual fortresses continued to hold out stubbornly against the conquerors.

There may also have been a master plan in the minds of some Ottoman strategists to extend the Ottoman Empire into Western Europe and Italy. Such a project, carefully calculated and pursued, might have worked out splendidly for the Turks had it been implemented by Suleiman in the sixteenth century. By the late seventeenth, as we shall see, things were very different.

Recall that the Thirty Years' War had devastated the Holy Roman Empire physically until 1648, and that the unity of the empire was subsequently greatly weakened in favor of the near independence of the states it comprised. Spain had begun to decline from its former position of European superpower and Catholic champion, while the new superpower, France, had been in the recent past willing to make alliances with the Turks when it suited her. French diplomacy saw the Catholic Hapsburgs as the main obstacle to French power. Similarly, the Hapsburgs were often preoccupied with their French enemy at the expense of organized campaigns against the Turks, and even papal policies fluctuated somewhat, depending on whether a given pope was inclined to favor the French or the Austrians. The continent that was formerly known as Christendom was now hopelessly divided, in short, and suffering from the effects of the greatest war it had yet experienced.

The Seventeenth Century

Despite fluctuations in the emphasis given at any particular moment to active promotion of war against the Turks, the papacy remained committed to the expulsion of the Ottomans from Christendom. This goal went hand in hand with the aims of the Counter-Reformation, particularly in Hungary. The Turks had been quick to appreciate the possibilities of the Reformation as a means of dividing and conquering their targets. They arranged religious debates between Protestants and Catholics in Hungary, in order to stimulate the antagonisms that would hinder national unity and resistance and play off one religion against another. Tragically, the combined effect on Hungary of Reformation propaganda, Turkish occupation, and lack of scope for an energetic Counter-Reformation on a national scale resulted in the permanent establishment of Lutheranism and Calvinism within the country. In the region of Transylvania, which managed to remain largely independent of Turkish rule, sometimes at the price of alliance with the enemy, the religious situation was worse. Besides mainstream Protestant heresies, a slippery heresy of many variations called Anti-Trinitarianism popped up, and even today the place is a center for Unitarianism.

In 1606, following several years of indecisive campaigns against the Turks by the Hapsburgs, to which the papacy contributed both large sums of money and tens of thousands of troops, a peace treaty was signed that held throughout the first half of the seventeenth century. There were still border skirmishes, and some fortresses and towns within occupied Hungary still heroically resisted capture, but no major campaigns occurred. The peace with the Turks allowed a certain Catholic restoration to develop in parts of the country, and major figures in the Hungarian Church — especially Cardinal Peter Pázmány — worked to obtain papal collaboration with the Hapsburgs in an all-out campaign against both Ottomans *and* Protestants, but in vain. (Recall that this fifty-year period saw the Puritan revolution in England and the Thirty Years' War on the continent, which absorbed the full attention of the European nations as well as of the popes.)

The situation changed in the second half of the century. With the cessation of the Thirty Years' War, the states of Europe were more inclined to consider the ever-present Turkish threat, particularly since internal developments at the Ottoman court had led to a more aggressive foreign policy. Papal dissatisfaction with the ecclesiastical policies of Louis XIV late in the century led to more cordial relations between the papacy and the Hapsburgs and a revival of the crusading spirit in Rome. Popes Alexander VII and Clement X supported the project of a new anti-Ottoman alliance with both military and diplomatic means. It was Pope Innocent XI, however, who orchestrated the last great crusade. Papal nuncios were sent all over Europe to promote the cause and neutralize the French threat to Austria, the leading crusader power.

Within the various regions of Hungary, the political and religious situation was unbelievably complex, and we need not sort it out here. Suffice it to say that strained relations between Hungarian leaders and the Hapsburg government were patched up. Another triumph of papal diplomacy was an alliance between Poland and Hapsburg Emperor Leopold I, which was to bring the Poles into the fray at a crucial point. Christendom was thus about as ready as it could be when the Turkish onslaught came in 1683. The great Turkish offensive may have been precipitated by the bizarre career of a Hungarian loose cannon named Imre Thököly, a zealous Calvinist who was twenty-two years old when he began a revolt to drive the Austrians out of northern Hungary in the late 1670s. The Turks, who had been unsuccessful in their attacks on Ukraine, followed his career with interest. When papal diplomacy succeeded in forging the Hungarian-Hapsburg reconciliation, Thököly decided to turn to the Turks for help and was welcomed with open arms. He was royally received by the pasha of Buda in 1682, and soon a joint army of Turks and rebels was off to conquer the whole country. They had great success, and Sultan Mehmed IV gave the traitor the title of King of Hungary and Croatia—as a vassal, of course, of the sultan.

The residents of the newly conquered regions found the occupiers far worse than the Austrian army they had replaced. Both the Turks and Thököly's men burned, enslaved, and ruined the regions they conquered, and embattled Emperor Leopold was forced to agree to a truce in late 1682 to gain time to build up his defensive coalition. The sultan, or at least his grand vizier, Kara Mustapha, used the pause to plan the completion of the grand design that had failed before the gates of Vienna in 1529. Sultan Mehmed IV, who ruled the Ottoman Empire in 1682, had come to the throne as a child and was used to leaving political affairs in the hands of the grand vizier, the traditional head of the government.

So great was the responsibility of the vizier that if he turned out to be a failure, he was not merely fired but executed. This had happened so often in Ottoman history that one would think there might have been a shortage of candidates for the post, but the Ottomans always seemed to find another hopeful for the job. In 1676, the death—a natural one—of a competent and successful grand vizier led to the appointment of his son-in-law, Kara Mustafa Pasha.

The Church Under Attack

As a minor, Sultan Mehmed had needed someone to run the state because he was too young to do so; when he grew up, he needed someone to run the state because he was far more interested in hunting and collecting falcons and dogs than in managing his realm. He could not seem to give up the chase and turn his attention to important affairs; periodically he promised to do so, but he always broke his promise and took off for the hunting field once again. (He was eventually imprisoned and deposed by his exasperated subjects.) Thus Kara Mustafa wielded even more power than was usual for the holder of the great office of grand vizier. Although he worked industriously to promote internal order and economic prosperity within the empire, his real desire was for military fame and glory. He dreamed of conquering Vienna, the gateway to Western Europe, although it is possible that he kept Mehmed in the dark about the details of this project until it was too late to stop it.

Meanwhile, Pope Innocent XI and his papal nuncios worked feverishly to forge an alliance of Austria, Poland, and various princes of the Holy Roman Empire before the Turks attacked again. It was on the very day—March 31—that Mehmed, Kara Mustafa, and a gigantic army set out for Hungary that Polish King Jan Sobieski joined the alliance. Mehmed and his immediate entourage stopped at Belgrade while Mustafa and the army moved on. Probably the grand vizier was relieved to shed his sultan, since now all the glory of which he was so certain would be his alone.

Once they reached Hungary, the Turkish forces were joined by the army of another Calvinist traitor from Transylvania, Prince Apafi, while Thököly attacked in western Slovakia. The offensive may have involved a Turkish force of as many as half a million men, although estimates vary wildly; there were a lot of them anyway, and it was certainly the strongest Turkish attack on Europe since the first siege of Vienna in the previous century. Kara Mustafa was first supposed to capture two Hungarian border fortresses, but his eagerness for military glory caused him to neglect these targets and move directly on Vienna, saying that if he took that city "all the Christians would obey the Ottomans."

As the huge army approached, the city's defense preparations were still incomplete, and Emperor Leopold and the court fled for safety. Had the Turks moved faster, they might have taken the city by storm, but their march was slow and they took days to surround the city and set up camp. The tens of thousands of tents, carts, and animals—including buffaloes and camels—must have been a daunting sight for the twelve thousand defenders to contemplate.

The traditional arrow was shot into the city bearing a message that demanded its surrender and offered safe-conduct to its inhabitants. The leader of the defense, Count Starhemberg, sent no reply, and so the siege commenced. Oddly enough, the Turks had not brought their heaviest artillery, which may indicate that Kara Mustafa's pretense of attacking only border fortresses had extended to the guns he had brought; bringing heavy cannon for a small-scale siege would have given away his real plans. Outgunned by the Viennese, the Turks began to mine the walls, but the defenders fought fiercely, and the siege dragged on. The delay demoralized the Turks, many of whom had already scooped up enough booty earlier in the campaign and now wanted only to go home. Kara Mustafa seems to have made two mistakes at this point: he hesitated to attack the city with full strength because, according to one Turkish historian, he was afraid the soldiers would get all the booty; he also ignored the fact that a major Christian army was on the way, to the relief of Vienna.

The siege had begun in mid-July. It was early September when the news came of the approach of an army of about seventy thousand, led by King Jan Sobieski and Prince Charles of Lorraine. It might have been stopped at the Danube, and Kara Mustafa supposedly had ordered his Tatar allies to do this, but for some reason—perhaps dislike of him—they did not comply. In any case it was another major mistake on his part not to do the job himself.

Meanwhile, within the city walls, the Viennese were desperate as the fall of the city began to seem imminent. The relief army attacked the Turks on September 12, 1683, and once again Mustafa muffed it. He ignored advice to use the disciplined and well-trained Janissary units and relied on an inadequate cavalry. The Turks fled, leaving at least ten thousand dead behind, as well as their entire camp and booty. It seems they had first killed their Christian prisoners except for five hundred children, who were liberated by the victorious allies. Sobieski sent a message to the pope imitating Julius Caesar's "I came, I saw, I conquered." As the Polish king put it, "I came, I saw, God conquered." Kara Mustafa, on the other hand, had not conquered, so he was strangled by order of the sultan when he arrived back in Belgrade with the remnants of his army.

The relief of Vienna was the beginning of a rapid rollback of the Turkish occupation forces, mainly under the brilliant leadership of a young commander in his twenties, Prince Eugene of Savoy. The ancient capital of Hungary, Buda, was liberated in 1686, and virtually the entire country was free of the Turks by 1689. The Venetians liberated Athens in 1687, and the key fort held by the Turks on the lower Danube, Belgrade, was freed in 1688.

At the crucial battle of Zenta, in 1697, a major Turkish offensive into Transylvania was met by Eugene of Savoy and his army. The date was September 11. The Turks lost about thirty thousand, killed in battle or drowned in the Tisza River, and several of the sultan's wives were captured. Eugene lost three hundred men. With the back of the Turkish army broken, the Ottomans were forced to sign the Treaty of Karlowitz with their adversaries, Russia, Poland, Austria, and Venice. By the terms of this treaty, Turkish attacks on Europe were brought to an end. There were still areas remaining under Turkish control, some of which would not be liberated until World War I, but the seventeenth-century crusade had freed much of occupied Central Europe and saved Europe from the threat that had hung over it for three hundred years. It was a spectacular success.

Catholic Thought and Culture in the Seventeenth Century: The Scientific Revolution

The Scientific Revolution is a somewhat heavy and involved topic, but it is vitally important for understanding much of our intellectual and cultural life today. The supposed opposition between science and religion; the current cult of everything "scientific"; the status of the scientist, whose pronouncements are received with the reverence and respect formerly given to saints or theologians; the craze for popular science; the preference given to scientific studies in schools; and the insertion of dubious "scientific" theories (such as those of Darwin, Kinsey, and Gould) into textbooks on just about anything—all these features are among the long-term consequences of the intellectual revolution that began in the seventeenth century.

The Church Under Attack

Before we take a deep breath and plunge into this complex and important series of developments, we should keep in mind three points. First, true science and technology are preeminently part of Western civilization; they flow from elements of the Western mentality such as the idea of *creation*. This truth includes as a corollary the concept of the goodness and intelligibility of nature; it is therefore an encouragement to man to study nature and make use of it. (If matter is evil, as in the religious mentality of some cultures, you don't study it; if it does not exist, as in others, you can't study it.) Secondly, the Church had always fostered scientific studies, and the major Western scientists such as Albertus Magnus, Roger Bacon, and Copernicus were all clerics; Galileo himself was a Catholic. Thirdly, Catholic Europe had excelled for centuries not only in theoretical science but also in the applied science we call technology: it was practical scientific innovations that made possible the transatlantic voyages of discovery, for example.

One other point must be stressed if we are to appreciate some of the truly revolutionary consequences of the changes that began in the seventeenth century, and it has to do with the very definition of science. For the Greeks and their Western cultural heirs, science meant "certain knowledge through causes" and included all types of investigation that produce *certitude*. Ancient and medieval thinkers took as the object of their study all of reality; not just the study of nature, but theology, philosophy, ethics, politics, and many other disciplines were called sciences. The sciences were arranged in a hierarchy according to their objects. Natural science was the lowest of the sciences because it dealt only with material things, while the sciences dealing with man, such as psychology and ethics, were higher. All these disciplines, however, deal with things that change. There were other sciences, higher still in the classical hierarchy, that deal with things that do not change: with being itself and with God. We call these sciences metaphysics and theology. Different methods were used for each discipline, but all were considered sciences, and they were approached through their *causes*.

This question of causality may seem a bit difficult, but it is crucial to understanding the gulf that opened in the Western mind, beginning in the seventeenth century, between how earlier thinkers had approached reality and how modern man looks at it. The Greeks and their intellectual descendants approached anything they wanted to know through four causes: material, formal, efficient, and final. They used the example of a statue to illustrate the operation of the causes. The *material* cause of a statue of Zeus is the marble from which it is made; its *formal* cause is the shape it takes, as an image of the god; the *efficient* cause is the sculptor who imposes the form on the marble; the *final* cause — the ultimate one, governing all the rest — is the purpose for which the statue is made: to be set up in a temple, for instance. In analyzing the operation of these causes in the objects they studied, the ancients accepted the fact that for most of the things they observed they would be able to determine only the first three causes; physics, biology, and astronomy, for instance, are incapable of providing information about final causality — their ultimate origin and purpose. For answers to those questions, the scientist turned to the higher sciences of metaphysics and theology.

Now how does the thinking of a modern scientist differ from what I have just described? It would seem to diverge in almost every way. To begin with, only the study of material things is now considered science, and it is generally much more highly esteemed than philosophy, theology, or any other field that the Greeks would have put at the top of their list. No modern thinker would consider philosophy or theology sciences or think of them as productive of any type of certitude whatever. In fact, a major consequence of the Scientific Revolution was the divorce of natural science from philosophy and theology and its eventual increase in status to the most highly valued field of study.

What about the four causes? Modern scientists still consider the matter and form of the things they investigate, as well as the proximate causes that affect them. What they repudiate, out of a sort of unspoken agnosticism, is final causality. It is ironic that what most interested Greek and Christian scholars was the true purpose of things—the ultimate Why—while contemporary thinkers are either totally uninterested in such questions or think that *qua* scientists they have no business thinking about them. The modern scientific mind, in fact, denies the reality of any nonmaterial cause and is thus reduced, should it be interested in final causality at all, to the futile exercise of looking for ultimate explanations in matter itself. I recall a modern textbook author who described how Roger Bacon accurately diagrammed the workings of the human eye and discovered the details of its operation. He remarked disparagingly, however, on Bacon's comment that the seven parts of the eye were like the seven gifts of the Holy Spirit, allowing supernatural light into the soul as natural light enters the body. For the modern writer, Bacon was dragging religion into what should have been a religion-proof scientific discussion; for Bacon, the delight of his discoveries included seeing the glory of the Creator reflected in the details of his creation.

We must not ignore the real breakthroughs that resulted from the Scientific Revolution, such as the development of the experimental method, the use of mathematics to formulate scientific propositions, and the invention and use of new scientific instruments. All this made possible enormous strides in modern science and technology. It could have occurred, however, without the rupture with the past and the radical change in mentality that accompanied the progress of the revolution. To sum up its long-term consequences, we can observe that the old worldview that saw distinction but not conflict between faith and reason, or between theology and biology, and that took all of reality, material and immaterial, as the object of its study, was destroyed. Science and philosophy parted company, and the work of old-fashioned thinkers such as Aristotle and Aquinas, who had harmonized the many disciplines, was rejected. The emphasis on final causality, the answer to the ultimate Why, was abandoned in favor of the descriptive *how*—how it operates, not why it is there in the first place. This shift has been described as a denial of the concept "that the world has a purpose more profound than its description." Natural science in the seventeenth century rose from the humblest area of research to its current position as standard for all others: science (narrowly defined) became the measure of all things, the final arbiter of truth, so that we now say, "Scientists tell us ..." or "A scientific study has shown ..." when we really want to clinch an argument. This new science is defined so as to exclude all causality that is not material. The scientist is the new high priest of arcane knowledge (and if he is a rocket scientist—well, you can't get wiser than that, can you?).

And it all started with Galileo. Here is the myth about the Galileo case that is still popular with people who should know better: Using a telescope, which he invented, Galileo discovered that the earth goes around the sun. The Church opposed him because of biblical passages that seemed to support geo-centricism and because Christianity had always been hostile toward science anyway. Hauled before the dreaded Inquisition, Galileo would not deny his findings. He was imprisoned in a dungeon, tortured, humiliated, and at length gave in. He signed the abject declaration they put before him and was sentenced to prison. As he tottered out of the court, a broken old man, he muttered, *"Eppur, si muove!"* ("And yet, it does move!") Thus did religious obscurantism triumph over science.

Every one of the statements in this account is false, and this legend was actually concocted more than a hundred years after the death of Galileo, when it began to be used to stigmatize the Church as anti-science. Here is the real story: Most ancient Greek scientists accepted the geocentric theory, elaborated by Ptolemy. It is apparently so accurate in accounting for the position of the stars that it is still useful for navigation; it was, in short, a theory that worked. Aristarchus proposed an alternative theory, the heliocentric, but it lacked the symmetry demanded by Greek thought (perfectly circular orbits, for example), and his calculations did not work very well. Hence, Ptolemy's remained the mainstream astronomical theory for many centuries. Dissatisfaction with it surfaced in the Middle Ages; inklings of gravity can be found in the work of some medieval physicists, and even St. Thomas wrote that "the hypotheses of the astrologers [astronomers] are not necessarily true; in employing them they seem to explain the facts, but one is not forced to believe that they are right; perhaps some scheme which is still unknown to man can serve to explain all the appearances of the stellar universe."

Thomas would have had no problem with someone proposing an alternative to the reigning Ptolemaic orthodoxy, and in the early sixteenth century the Catholic cleric Copernicus did so. The Catholic Church allowed the publication of his work, but Calvin and Luther (who called Copernicus an ass) condemned it on scriptural grounds. Some of the technical difficulties with Copernicus's theory were dealt with by the German astronomer Johannes Kepler, who thus made the heliocentric theory more plausible. Kepler, however, was persecuted by the Protestants in Tubingen and had to flee to the Jesuits for protection in 1596.

Enter Galileo. Obviously, he did not invent the heliocentric theory, but he championed it strongly as not merely a theory but a fact. He was a better physicist than he was an astronomer, and astronomically he was often on shaky ground. He did not invent the telescope, although he did improve on it. He did not discover sunspots either. He was wildly wrong about the "moons of Jupiter" and the movement of the tides (as at least one pope tried to explain to him) and thought comets were an optical illusion. Catholic scholars of the time may be forgiven for refusing to admit Galileo's version of heliocentrism as a fact, especially since differently formulated theories had not yet been disproved.

Galileo, however, with his oversize ego and fiery temperament, became more and more intransigent as his theory met with increasing skepticism. Pope Urban VIII, once so much of a Galileo fan that he wrote an ode in his honor and showed him other signs of favor, suggested that his friend support the Copernican system without insisting on its absolute truth because it had not been proved. Galileo's response was to write his *Dialogue Concerning the Two Chief World Systems — Ptolemaic and Copernican*, in which he places the pope's words in the mouth of a dunce. This amounted to public mockery of a man who was not only pope, but also a fellow Florentine almost as fiery and hot-tempered as Galileo himself.

In publicly trumpeting his theory as fact despite its apparent contradiction of Scripture, Galileo took it upon himself to interpret Scripture his own way, in spite of his lack of training as an exegete. "I commenced to play the theologian," he said, commenting on an after-dinner conversation with royalty and scholars. He was ordered to pipe down but continued to stir up trouble until at length he found he had gone too far. Galileo was summoned to Rome to answer to a committee of cardinals. (In contradiction to pictures you might have seen of a trembling old man in the midst of a mob of bloodthirsty Inquisitors, those present were exactly four: Galileo, two officials, and a secretary.) The grounds for complaint against the astronomer were: that if stated as a fact, his theory could be seen as contradicting passages in Scripture and upsetting the faith of simple people; the public insult to the pope; the fact that his assertions were not proven; and his apparent claim to the right to decide what Scripture meant in the light of his unproven theory.

During the investigation, Galileo lived in a Vatican palace with a servant, his food and wine provided by the Tuscan ambassador. He was never in prison and was neither tortured nor in fear of torture. The tribunal of cardinals read and voted on the report of the two officials who dealt with the accused; three refused to vote, and the pope never confirmed the verdict. As Descartes remarked, the action taken against Galileo was merely the disciplinary action of a committee. Galileo was ordered to remain in his home in Tuscany, where he lived for ten peaceful years, during which he did his best work—on motion and gravity—which would later be built upon by Newton.

The Seventeenth Century

This whole sordid episode, the basis for the supposed opposition between science and religion, need never have happened at all if Galileo had been as reasonable as his opponents. Here is St. Robert Bellarmine's position:

> I say that if there were a true demonstration that the sun is at the center of the world and the earth in the third heaven, and that the sun does not circle the earth but the earth circles the sun, then one would have to proceed with great care in explaining the Scriptures that appear contrary, and say rather that we do not understand them than that what is demonstrated is false. But I will not believe that there is such a demonstration, until it is shown to me.

As Arthur Koestler remarks in *The Sleepwalkers,* "Galileo did not want to bear the burden of proof; for the crux of the matter is … that he had no proof." In discussing the sunspot problem, the author goes further, accusing Galileo of "contempt for the intelligence of his contemporaries," and concluding that "impostures like Galileo's are rare in the annals of science."[4]

England and Ireland

Throughout the seventeenth century, the vitality of Catholic culture was inspired and stimulated by the Counter-Reformation, which began, as we have seen, in the previous century. It would seem pretty difficult to contribute much to Catholic civilization with your back to the wall and the bloodhounds hunting you down—the situation of many English Catholics—or with a fanatical army trying to wipe you out of existence—the

---

[4] Arthur Koestler, *The Sleepwalkers,* 443, 486.

situation in Ireland, yet England and Ireland produced noble characters and saints and bequeathed to the Catholic heritage numerous examples of gallantry and heroism.

To take Ireland first, we can see in the Irish reaction to the English attempt to destroy their Catholic Faith (and their Catholic selves) a number of parallels with the situation of Catholics under the Roman emperor Diocletian. There is the same mobilizing of the whole power of the state to crush Catholic resistance, the same stubborn determination of numerous ordinary believers, as well as the clergy, who were particularly targeted for death, to hold to their Faith at all costs. There were similar inducements for apostasy offered too: a pinch of incense to the Roman gods in the first, second, third, and part of the fourth centuries could buy you your life and the favor of the state; allegiance to the newly created religion of the English state in the sixteenth, seventeenth, eighteenth, and part of the nineteenth centuries would do the same.

A striking example of the willingness of the Irish to choose extreme hardship and even exile over capitulation occurred following the victory of William of Orange over the Irish forces and the drawing up of the Treaty of Limerick in 1691. The defeated Irish soldiers were invited to join the English army. If they did not want to do that, they could choose exile from Ireland and service in the army of France. Two standards—the English and the French—were therefore set up in a field and the soldiers summoned to advance and make their choice. Some 15,000 men marched up to the two markers, and there they turned to the left or to the right. When all had chosen, it was found that some 14,000 had chosen Catholic France and exile, while only 1,046 chose England. The exiles left for the continent accompanied by about 10,000 women and children;

most served in the armies of France or other Catholic powers and never saw their homeland again. Some accounts say that their famous General Sarsfield, falling mortally wounded on a foreign battlefield, looked at the blood flowing from his wound and bewailed the fact that it was not being shed for Ireland.

As for the Irish at home, driven from their land, subject to laws possibly even more cruel and unjust than any Roman edicts, how were they to keep and pass on the Faith? They were forbidden to school their children as they wished, but like Roman Christians, they found ways of doing it anyway. Even under the earlier Puritan regime of Cromwell, they had kept up the teaching of children despite the penalties of death or slavery in the West Indies imposed on schoolmasters. The ranks of their clergy were decimated, and what priests managed to survive were constantly on the run. St. Oliver Plunkett, the first of the Irish martyrs to be beatified, had promoted education in Ireland during his tenure as Primate of Ireland in the late 1660s and 1670s. When a wave of anti-Catholic hysteria erupted in England with the so-called Popish Plot (an alleged Catholic conspiracy to kill King Charles II, fabricated by Titus Oates in 1678), he was forced into hiding and finally arrested for treason in 1679. He was taken to England, convicted of promoting the Catholic Faith, hanged, drawn, and quartered; his was one of thirty-five executions engineered by fanatical English government ministers, despite the weak opposition of the king, who was persuaded to authorize the executions for the sake of peace: "I sign with tears in my eyes."

The famous "hedge schools" began in reaction to the Penal Laws that followed William II's victory over the Irish, which, among dozens of other prohibitions, forbade Catholics from teaching either in public or in private. The Protestants set up schools, of course, but Irish parents rejected this clear attempt to destroy their children's faith. The result was that Irish bards and schoolmasters taught Irish children in secret; not just behind hedges but also in barns, ditches, and anywhere they could find a secluded spot. Education went underground as the Church had gone into the catacombs under the Romans.

Although the curriculum varied from place to place, hedge-school pupils were taught religion, Irish history and traditions, reading, writing, arithmetic, and even Latin and Greek. A traveler to a remote village in Ireland in the eighteenth century was astounded to hear the villagers bargaining over the price of cows in Greek. Thus, like Roman parents, Irish mothers and fathers employed such teachers as they could find to educate their children secretly—and this for well over a century. They managed in this way to preserve not only the Faith, but also the heritage of Catholic civilization, much as the Europeans of the Dark Ages preserved literacy and the Faith at great cost to themselves, until the dark time was past.

The situation of seventeenth-century English Catholics differed from that of the Irish, and in some ways it was more difficult. The English recusants did not have the comfort of a national unity in the face of invasion and tyranny by foreign heretics. It was often their neighbors, in fact, who were their enemies, and this also recalls the predicament of Catholics in imperial Rome. If a Roman citizen did not send his children to pagan schools, did not participate in pagan worship, and was otherwise "different" from his fellows, he could be spied upon and denounced to the authorities. (The Irish had their "informers" and their personal enemies too, but they were not the bulk of the population, as in England.) Catholics in England were barred from holding many public offices, heavily fined for not attending Anglican services, and subjected to various other penalties throughout the century, which varied according to the government in power.

Often Catholics were married to non-Catholics, and this gave rise to delicate problems of conscience in times of persecution. Women had few rights in English law and tended to be targeted as religious subversives less frequently than their husbands. They played an important role in hiding priests, teaching catechism to children and servants, and sometimes dying for their Faith. Since they were seen as weak and subservient, any assertion of their spiritual independence was regarded by the authorities as revolutionary. Antonia Fraser, in her book on the Gunpowder Plot, cites *A Treatise of Christian Renunciation*, written by Father Henry Garnet, one of the English martyrs canonized in 1970. This work examined the problems of families under persecution, with examples from the early Church, and St. Henry's advice to wives with Protestant husbands included the statement, "Your husbands over your souls have no authority, and over your bodies but a limited power." King James remarked indignantly that, unlike Protestant women who were submissive to their husbands, "their [Catholic women's] consciences must ever be commanded and overruled by their Romish God as it pleases him." So might Diocletian have put it.

These parallels between the situation of Christians in ancient Rome and conditions imposed by the Reformation in both England and Ireland are striking. Graham Greene, in his introduction to *The Autobiography of a Hunted Priest*, by Father John Gerard, S.J., who was implicated along with Father Garnet in the Gunpowder Plot, refers to the terrible scenes of torture and martyrdom, trials and condemnations, heroes, and sadists such as the torturer Topcliffe that characterized Elizabethan and Jacobean England. He asks:

> Isn't there one whole area ... that we miss even in Shakespeare's huge world of comedy and despair? The kings speak, the adventurers speak ... the madmen and the lovers, the soldiers and the poets, but the martyrs are quite silent—one might say that the Christians are silent, except for the diplomatic tones of a Wolsey or Pandulpho or the sudden flash of conscience in Hamlet's uncle at prayers.... One might have guessed from Shakespeare's plays that there was a vast vacuum where the Faith had been—the noise and bustle of pilgrimages has been stilled: we come out of the brisk world of Chaucer into the silence of Hamlet's court after the Prince's departure.... An old Rome has taken the place of the Christian Rome—the pagan philosophers and the pagan gods seem to have returned.... How far removed are they from the routine of the torture chamber.

Fortunately, Father Gerard's autobiography lets us enter the real world of the early seventeenth century, and it is a chilling one.

Charles I was not a Catholic, but he gained the support of Catholics because of his Catholic queen and his disinclination to persecute them. Many of his political ideas, expressed at his trial and elsewhere, reflect the traditional Catholic concepts of legitimacy and responsible hierarchical government. With Cromwell, of course, that political philosophy was first suppressed, then briefly and feebly resurrected under the last two Stuart kings, and then supplanted by the triumph of Protestant parliamentarianism.

The Seventeenth Century

With the accession of Charles II, one of the major figures of the Counter-Reformation appears in England: St. Claude de la Colombière. This famed spiritual director and confidant of St. Margaret Mary (whom we will meet later) was drawn into the ominous religious atmosphere of England by an odd series of circumstances. Charles II had a Catholic mother and counted a number of Catholics as his friends, as he himself recounts in *An Account of the Preservation of King Charles II, after the Battle of Worcester, Drawn Up by Himself.* In particular, he was indebted to a faithful priest, Father Huddleston, who once saved his life; Charles told him, "If it please God to restore me my kingdom, the Catholics will have less need to live in hiding." When Charles lay dying, still undecided about entering the Church, his brother brought Father Huddleston to his bedside: "Sire," said James, "this good man once saved your life. He now comes to save your soul." And he did.

It was due to Charles's friendship toward Catholics, although the Protestants in his government fought him all the way each time he tried to ease Catholics' pariah status, that St. Claude was invited to come to England as chaplain to the wife of Charles's Catholic brother, James II. This wife, a fifteen-year-old Italian princess named Mary Beatrice, was at first appalled at the marriage suddenly arranged for her just as she was about to enter a Visitation convent and declared she would rather "cast herself into the fire" than agree to it. It took nothing less than a letter from Pope Clement X to reconcile her to her change of vocation. In his letter, the Holy Father urged her to think of the good that could come from her marriage: "The true religion, which has been forced to go underground in this land for fear of persecution, might be restored by you, and her ancient luster renewed." Mary Beatrice wept and lamented that she had not been born a commoner who could choose her fate, but in the end she acquiesced. Her letters to the Visitation nuns she had hoped to join give a vivid picture of her difficult adjustment to her new life: the cold English weather made her ill and depressed her, and court life was not to her taste. On the other hand, "my Lord the Duke is an excellent man. He loves me very much, and leaves nothing undone to please me. He is besides so solidly grounded in our holy religion (which he professes like a good Catholic) that he will not give it up for anything in the world."

James II was indeed a much more competent and intelligent man than many books portray him. He was considered a great military captain by those who had served with him and was both creator and grand admiral of the English fleet. He was also brave, both on the battlefield and off it. When his brother King Charles tried to persuade him to take the oath required by the new Test Act, which declared Transubstantiation to be idolatry, James would not accept his brother's argument that it was merely a matter of form. "I would rather die!" James thundered and promptly resigned all his posts, including that of admiral of his beloved fleet. This, as a recent historian has noted, deprived Charles of the valuable assistance of "the most capable of all the Stuarts."

When St. Claude arrived in London as preacher to the Duchess of York, Mary Beatrice, in 1676, he found himself confined by the religious situation to a small cold room in St. James Palace and the small palace chapel. His letters describe his impressions of the place, and like Mary Beatrice, he suffered from the cold. British subjects were theoretically forbidden to attend services at the Catholic chapels allowed for diplomats and other foreigners like Mary Beatrice, but St. Claude observed that a number of English Catholics managed to come to his chapel, and it seems to have been a major center of Catholic activity. He seems to have been one of the greatest preachers of his day, and perhaps of any day. He fell victim to the anti-Catholic hysteria aroused by the Titus Oates Plot in 1678 and was imprisoned for two weeks, escaping possible execution due to an attack of consumption that eventually resulted in his release and return to France. He died in 1682, six years before the overthrow and exile of the duke and duchess, briefly king and queen of England, whom he had so faithfully directed and served.

A historian has written, "The restored Stuarts proved unable to deal with British anti-Catholic feeling, a prejudice so firmly entrenched in the British psyche as to be impervious to reason, blandishment or power." Yet despite the inauspicious religious climate, or perhaps—as with the Christians of Rome—because of it, seventeenth-century Catholics in England and Ireland kept the Faith and died for it in large numbers. They also kept Catholic education alive, sharpened their skills in apologetics to meet new attacks on Catholicism, and bequeathed to the Catholic heritage examples of great virtue and heroism. We have much to thank them for.

France

In French culture, the seventeenth century is known as the "classical" period, during which great artistic creations were produced in almost every area. The Palais Royal and the palace of Versailles exemplified the classical style in architecture, as the works of Poussin did in painting. Classical literature ranged from the great dramas of Corneille and Racine, to the comedies of Molière, to the poetry of Malherbe, the *Fables* of La

Fontaine, the letters of Madame de Sévigné, and the works of numerous other writers in many genres.

For Catholic spirituality, the period is even richer, since some of the greatest saints of all time were French subjects of either Louis XIII or Louis XIV. Catholic intellectual life was so rich, varied, intense, and sometimes fraught with controversy that it is impossible to describe it adequately here. Two outstanding clerics, although not saints, were major figures in the religious and literary life of their day. Jacques-Bénigne Bossuet was a great bishop as well as one of the greatest orators in Christendom; his friend, until controversy strained their friendship, was Bishop François de Salignac de la Mothe-Fénelon, described by Antoine Degert, in a *Catholic Encyclopedia* article as "one of the most attractive, brilliant, and puzzling figures that the Catholic Church has ever produced." Bossuet and Fénelon both combated Jansenism, a slippery, multiform heresy that denied free will and the possibility of resisting grace, something like Calvinism. Their friendship came to grief over the case of an influential lady, Madame Guyon, who promoted a spirituality in which some detected evidence of Quietism: mysticism of such excessive passivity of mind and soul that one would not even desire heaven or make acts of faith, hope, and charity. Madame Guyon submitted obediently when some of her ideas were condemned, but Fénelon went on arguing the case and the interpretation of certain texts, and was forcefully opposed by Bossuet. At length some of Fénelon's propositions were also condemned, but this did not prevent him—after his submission—from continuing his many valuable works and pursuing the struggle against Jansenism until his death.

The real glory of France in the seventeenth century is, of course, her saints. When the century dawned, the future St.

The Seventeenth Century

Vincent de Paul was twenty years old and his peasant family had just had the satisfaction of seeing him ordained a priest. A few years later, young Father Vincent came under the influence of the saintly Cardinal Bérulle, founder of the French branch of St. Philip Neri's Oratory, and began to lead a life of more fervent prayer and penance. Of Bérulle he was to say later, "He is one of the most saintly priests I have known," while St. Francis de Sales described him as everything he would have liked to be himself. Cardinal Bérulle's death seems to have been particularly blessed: he died while saying Mass.

St. Vincent's later career defies summation. The peasant priest acquired an international reputation for his vast and saintly correspondence, conferences, retreats, and uplifting influence throughout the Church in France; even Bossuet attended his "days of recollection." He is probably best known for his dynamic and pioneering work in relieving the distress of the poorest of the poor. He seems to have been everywhere at once, establishing "charity confraternities" to help the poor all over France, founding the religious congregations of the Vincentians and the Sisters of Charity, and working for the redemption of slaves and the relief of prisoners condemned to the galleys. And then there was that voluminous correspondence. Somehow he did it all before his death in 1660.

In the same year, a few months before the death of St. Vincent, his great spiritual daughter, St. Louise de Marillac, also died. She might have seemed an unlikely woman to end her life serving and nursing the poor. She was born into the aristocracy and married a secretary to the queen. He became ill, and while she was caring for him, two years before he died, she had a vision of herself in a religious community, caring for the poor. In the vision she saw an unknown man whom she would later recognize as St. Vincent de Paul. Once she had met him, they worked together on the "charity confraternities," and Louise began to teach young women who came to her about the work she was doing. This group of women would become the Sisters of Charity, with a worldwide apostolate. Some of the Sisters became martyrs in the French Revolution and in the overseas mission fields. (St. Elizabeth Ann Seton established the order in the young United States.) At the time, the idea of religious women leaving their convents and going into homes to nurse the sick and to care for children and the poor was a novelty and met with some opposition. So great was the need, however, that the Sisters were soon in demand to staff hospitals and other institutions. They never forgot that their function was apostolic, not merely material; in their first year, they were said to have converted over seven hundred souls, including Lutherans, Calvinists, and Turks. Later on, they could include the souls of soldiers they nursed on the battlefield and brought back to the Faith.

St. Francis de Sales should be at least mentioned here, although he died rather early in the century (1622). In his fifty-six years, he had been bishop of Geneva, a major figure of the Counter-Reformation who worked tirelessly for the conversion of the Calvinists, immortal author of *Introduction to the Devout Life*, *Treatise on the Love of God*, and other works, and founder—with St. Jane de Chantal—of the Visitation Order. We will meet the Visitation again when we come to one of the greatest saints it produced.

The life of St. John Eudes spanned much of the seventeenth century, from his birth in 1601 to his death in 1680. He was one of the greatest domestic missionaries in French history, preaching more than a hundred missions all over France. He also devoted himself to the education of priests, founded a religious congregation, and worked for the relief of the poor and the sick. He contributed providentially to the growth of devotion to the Heart of Mary and the Sacred Heart of Jesus by promoting both devotions and writing the Mass and Office for the feast of the Holy Heart of Mary (first celebrated in 1648) and the Sacred Heart of Jesus (1672).

The older religious orders furnished many of the saints of the century. St. Francis Regis, a Jesuit of deeply mortified life, exercised a dual apostolate. He was a great missionary and confessor, credited with regaining many thousands of souls for Christ through his indefatigable preaching and administration of the sacrament of Penance. He also engaged in the often thankless and sometimes dangerous work of reclaiming prostitutes from their evil lives and finding them legitimate means of earning a living. His presence in the urban slums put his life in danger more than once, but it seems his courage and the mere expression on his face saved him: the words *brightness* and *shining* are used by biographers to describe his countenance on these occasions. He died exhausted by his prodigious labors at the age of forty-three.

One of his fellow Jesuits died at only thirty-nine. St. Isaac Jogues, the first priest to set foot in Manhattan, is perhaps the best known of the eight French Jesuits who were hideously tortured and martyred in the 1640s; they have been canonized as the North American Martyrs. Their stories are well known and will not be given here. While they were dying in present-day New York, a French Ursuline nun, Blessed Marie of the Incarnation, was studying Indian languages in Quebec in order to convert and instruct Indian children. In France, she had been the young and unhappy wife of a merchant until his death two years after their marriage. She then devoted herself to her son, and when he was grown she entered the Ursuline Order. (The son became a saintly Benedictine and wrote his mother's biography.) As an Ursuline, Marie was able to follow her strong attraction for work in the missions; she also left some writings, including a chronicle of her life in the New World.

Thus France, in one of her most glorious ages, gave a prodigious number of saints to the Church, as well as a legion of other holy men and women, only some of whom have been beatified. (Father Marquette, for example, is thought of in this country as an early explorer, although he is far more important as a heroic Jesuit missionary.) Kateri Tekakwitha, the Lily of the Mohawks, was not French, but she certainly absorbed French spirituality, along with the language, from her Jesuit mentors.

A seventeenth-century French saint whom we have met in an earlier chapter, St. Claude la Colombière, is the Jesuit whom God deigned to use in an unprecedented divine intervention in human history: Jesus' apparitions to St. Margaret Mary Alacoque, in which he requested not only the promotion of the Sacred Heart devotion but its public profession by the King of France.

The story of St. Margaret Mary is both touching and harrowing. The tribulations she suffered in her early years did not end when she entered the Visitation Order, founded by St. Francis de Sales. Particularly after her apparitions began, she was subject to the incomprehension of her spiritual directors and sometimes to excessive and inexplicable hostility from her fellow nuns. There was even an occasion on which the other nuns ganged up on her and dragged her through the corridors by her hair, which smacks of diabolical provocation, but the confidante of the Sacred Heart endured it all.

The Seventeenth Century

Our Lord promised to send her his "faithful servant and perfect friend" to help her, and he kept his promise. When St. Claude la Colombière was sent to the Visitation as confessor in 1675, St. Margaret Mary finally found someone who could understand what was going on in her soul. She told him about our Lord's complaint that his Heart, which had so loved men, received from them only coldness. She revealed the mission given her to promote the feast of the Sacred Heart, the five First Fridays, and the holy hour on the preceding Thursday night, and he became her faithful collaborator in the enterprise. Although he was sent to England the following year (as we saw in a previous chapter) he continued to direct St. Margaret Mary by letter. Eventually, her community came to appreciate her. She was even appointed novice mistress and was able to institute celebrations in honor of the Sacred Heart before her death in 1690, eight years after that of her holy collaborator.

Our Lord's demands were eventually carried out, except for one. On June 17, 1689, the year before her death, St. Margaret Mary received this message from our Lord:

> Make known to the eldest son of my Sacred Heart that, as his temporal birth was obtained by devotion to my Holy Infancy, so will he obtain his birth into grace and eternal glory by consecrating himself to my adorable Heart. It wants to triumph over his and, through him, over the hearts of the great ones of the earth. It wants to reign in his palace, be painted on his standards, and engraved on his arms, so that they may be victorious over all his enemies. It wants to bring low these proud and stubborn heads and make him triumphant over all the enemies of holy Church.

The Church Under Attack

The king in question was Louis XIV, whose birth had been the result of fervent and public prayer. The message apparently reached him, but he did nothing about it. Perhaps he was afraid of ridicule, or his confessor discouraged him. Whatever the reason, we should notice the date of the request; we will meet that ominous date of June 17 one hundred years later, when the consequences of the royal refusal will begin to unfold.

I have not discussed the non-French saints of this century; to do so would require several more chapters. We should keep in mind, however, that the fruits of the Counter-Reformation were produced throughout the world. One of the most extraordinary of saints, St. Joseph Cupertino, was wonder-working in Italy during this century. St. Martin de Porres died in Lima in 1639, and St. Peter Claver ministered to the slaves imported into South America until his death in 1654. In Japan, the persecution of 1617–1632 produced more than two hundred martyrs of several nationalities and religious orders.

There are so many saints from this century that it is difficult to tally them up. It is as if God was giving to Christendom a truly extraordinary number of workers capable of building up the kingdom of the Sacred Heart on earth—dependent, however, in his inscrutable providence, on the cooperation of the French king. Absent that, we will find in the following century not only a dearth of French saints but also the most catastrophic developments for the Church and for civilization that had yet occurred in history.

Chapter 3

The Eighteenth Century

For the historian, the shadow of the Age of Revolution, which began with the American and French Revolutions of the late eighteenth century, lies over the whole period of the 1700s, although many of the events of the time were more reflections of the previous period than previews of the gruesome future.

In general, the eighteenth was a century of war among the European great powers, while fighting against the Turks also continued sporadically. France was the dominant power until 1713, when its strength declined and no one state dominated European affairs. Two new states — Prussia and Russia — came to prominence; along with Austria, they developed strong, centralized governments under rulers who were called enlightened despots. They would evolve into the political and ideological powder kegs of the twentieth century. Finally, England (known as Great Britain following the union with Scotland in 1707) came to lead the world in economic development and commerce.

The middle years of the century would see new inventions and agricultural improvements that foreshadowed the mechanization of industry and the Industrial Revolution.

The Church Under Attack

Obviously, there is material here for several volumes, and the best we can do is give brief sketches of each major state during the eighteenth century, mentioning the position of the Church in each, and discuss a few of the great figures of the era. I will leave France for a later chapter, because its eighteenth-century history leads directly into the Revolution. To begin with England, then, a shift in the ruling family occurred early in the century. Queen Anne (that disloyal daughter of James II who joined her sister in overthrowing him) died childless in 1714. The parliamentary masters of the country, scrambling to come up with a successor, hit upon a somewhat distant German relative from the Hanover family. He did not even speak English and was more concerned with affairs back in Germany than in England—which suited Parliament just fine. He was succeeded in 1727 by his son, George II, who spoke English with an accent and was in turn succeeded by George III, the mentally unbalanced monarch who had the misfortune to rule—if it can be called that, since Parliament by now called all the shots—during the revolt of the American colonies.

Two political factions that had emerged in the seventeenth century had become political parties by the eighteenth: Whigs and Tories. The former were largely nobles and merchants who favored Parliament to advance their economic interests; they tended to loathe Catholics, dislike Anglicanism, and include religious dissenters in their ranks. The Tories were mostly Anglican landowners, clergy, and other conservatives eager to keep both state and church out of the hands of Puritans and Catholics, but above all to avoid the civil war that had earlier haunted the country. They saw hereditary monarchy as the best hope of stability. Some Tories known as Jacobites even favored the exiled heirs of Catholic King James II who were living in

The Eighteenth Century

France: James III, "the Old Pretender," and his son Charles, "the Young Pretender," known as Bonnie Prince Charlie. There were two risings in favor of the banished Stuarts, in 1715 and 1745. The disastrous Battle of Culloden in 1745 saw the defeat of Prince Charles and his allies, including Scots Highlanders and Irish volunteers, and the ruin of the Catholic Jacobite cause. An appallingly savage repression followed, carried out by Duke William of Cumberland and his cronies; there is too much to tell about it here, but several websites exist detailing this significant and melancholy event. (Peter Watkins's 1964 BBC video, *Culloden*, is unforgettable for its innovative portrayal of the horrors of this conflict.) It is barely possible that if Charles had followed advice to march on London he could have succeeded, which makes the 1745 rising all the more intriguing.

In other areas, rampant bribery and corruption in Parliament seem to have been the focus of reform movements, but there were plenty of worse abuses. Numerous crimes, some as trivial as cutting down an apple tree or stealing a shilling, were punishable by death. Economic dislocation reduced farm workers to practical serfdom, while children were carted off to factories and the indigent shut up in workhouses. We will treat this topic more fully later. Early in the century Catholics were still barred from political life, Irish Catholics were still oppressed, and Quakers could still be imprisoned. By the last two decades, however, such legal penalties were increasingly eliminated; life imprisonment for priests, for example, was abolished.

International wars involving Great Britain occurred at intervals throughout the century. The War of the Spanish Succession (1702–1713) ended in a defeat for France and a corresponding increase in the size of the British Empire. Similarly, the Seven Years' War (1756–1763—although a rash young George Washington had precipitated it two years earlier in America)—again saw Great Britain profit territorially at the expense of France. Then came the war of independence fought by the North American colonies with the crucial help of France. (Great Britain lost.)

Moving east, and skipping France for the time being, since we will be spending some time there later, we will look quickly at Russia and Prussia and end with a pleasant visit to a genuinely good, competent, and dedicated wife and mother, who also happens to be one of the great Catholic rulers of history. To take the ruler of Russia first: Peter the Great (1682–1725) was not especially good, but he was competent—ruthlessly so. Reviewing pre-Peter Russian history, we recall that the first Russian state was founded by Vikings in the 800s and Christianized from Byzantium in the 900s. The Mongols conquered it in the 1200s, and it was not until the fifteenth century that the princes of Moscow were able to overthrow them and organize a powerful northern Russian state. Lurching through internal turmoil and foreign invasion, the Muscovite state survived into the eighteenth century as an autocratic, backward country based on serfdom, in which few were literate and cruelty and murder at court were common occurrences. (Peter, at the age of ten, witnessed a particularly horrific example of this following his father's death in 1682 and hated the Moscow Kremlin ever after.)

Peter reigned from 1682 to 1725, but of course he had to spend quite a few of those years growing up (up and up, actually, since he was eventually about seven feet tall) and learning all he could about the problems of Russia. He was consumed with a desire to drag his country into the modern world whether it wanted to go or not. When he visited Western Europe, rulers were appalled at his uncouth manners but they furnished him with naval technology and other means of modernizing Russia. In place of the hated Moscow, he built a new capital on the forbidding north coast—St. Petersburg—at the cost of numerous deaths from harsh working conditions. It is a dream of light, pastel, European architecture, having nothing in common with the gloomy fortress of the Kremlin. Russian ladies had to hold salons and discuss Enlightenment ideas, while noblemen who refused to update their looks risked having the czar himself modernize their faces with his scissors, cutting off their beards. Peter had little use for religion and treated the Russian Church harshly; secular French culture, he thought, was what Russia needed.

Peter is credited with putting Russia on the map as a European power, both by conquering former Swedish territory and modernizing his country willy-nilly. For this he was given the title "the Great." We can skip the period between his reign and that of the next "Great," who comes on the scene in 1796, when a childless Russian empress, Elizabeth, arranged a marriage between her German nephew Peter and a German princess named Catherine. The two could not stand each other, and since Peter was so childish that he spent most of his time playing with toy soldiers, we can understand how young Catherine must have felt. She also felt that he was in her way to absolute power. Aided by one of her numerous alleged lovers, she had him murdered and took the throne herself; because she professed Enlightenment ideas while ruling autocratically, she is known as an enlightened despot. The naive philosophe Diderot visited her court to discuss all the reforms that could be made in the lives of the Russian people, but he had to acknowledge at last that she implemented none of them. In fact, as Edward

The Church Under Attack

Crankshaw has written, "She brutalized the Russian peasants to a degree for centuries unsurpassed." One way or another she increased Russian territory by two hundred thousand square miles and seventeen million people and is therefore called "the Great." She seems something of a moral monster, a view apparently shared by her son, who was so opposed to women rulers in Russia that there has never been another one. I know of one small incident to her credit. When Diderot was dying in poverty, he was forced to sell his much-loved library to get money. Catherine offered to buy the collection and sent him the price; then she let him keep his precious books.

Thus Russia became a significant and powerful player in European history in the eighteenth century. So did the formerly obscure state of Prussia in northeast Germany, which had made territorial gains from the Thirty Years' War (1618–1648) and benefited from a series of rulers—all named Frederick—who streamlined the government and built up the military until Prussia had both a disproportionately large and extremely well-trained army.

Frederick William I, father of the eighteenth-century ruler we are trying to get to (also named, of course, Frederick) further modernized the Prussian army. This "Soldier King" was unfortunately afflicted with the same mental disorder as George III of England, which caused him to behave unpredictably. He was obsessed with forming a group of six- to seven-foot-tall Potsdam Grenadiers and paid to have men of this height kidnapped. (Once it backfired, when the tall man who was snatched as he entered a coach turned out to be the French ambassador; an international incident was narrowly averted.) Frederick William I also imposed an extremely frugal and Spartan regime on his government and household.

The Eighteenth Century

All this was a torment for his sensitive, artistic son Frederick, who played the flute and wrote music that is still performed. He grew up to become a cynical ruler who professed Enlightenment ideas and brought Voltaire to his Potsdam court. He implemented mercantilism (government regulation of the economy), the reigning economic theory of the time, trying to make Prussia self-sufficient to the point of growing its own tobacco—which somehow didn't work. It seems that tobacco does not flourish near the Baltic Sea, but an intellectual idealist like Fred tried it anyway. He kept serfdom, disliked Jews, and was not religious, but he paradoxically protected Catholics and welcomed the Jesuits—whose intellects he admired—after the order was suppressed. His wife drifted away, and he seems not to have cared too much; he is buried with his beloved greyhounds, which on his tombstone are called his only friends.

What makes Fred an enlightened despot is his combining of liberal ideas with despotism; what gives him the title of "the Great" is his military genius, which placed Prussia firmly among the great powers of Europe and set it on the path that would lead to a unified, militaristic Germany in the following century. We cannot follow Fred's brilliant tactics through the course of the War of the Austrian Succession and the Seven Years' War, although both wars were in part duels between him and his great Catholic antagonist, Maria Theresa, whom we will now meet.

When Charles VI, Holy Roman Emperor and King of Austria, died in 1740, he left only a twenty-three-year-old daughter, a bankrupt treasury, an ill-equipped army, and promises he had naively extracted from neighboring countries that they would allow her to rule in peace. So began the War of the Austrian Succession, which became a global war that took some four hundred thousand civilian lives. Frederick II, who would become the young empress's great rival, invaded the important Austrian territory of Silesia, while several other neighbors began sharpening their swords to carve up the rest of her realm. In a dramatic move, the lovely young empress fled to Hungary and charmed the nobility into coming to her rescue. When the war ended eight years later, she was forced to accept the loss of Silesia but had managed to keep her throne and the rest of Austrian territory.

Carlton Hayes has written of Maria Theresa that "love of her subjects was not a theory with her—it was a religious duty." She believed in serving her people and would go in disguise among them to assess their real needs. She reduced taxes on the poor, reformed the courts, began the emancipation of the serfs, established schools for the poor, implemented public health measures, and much more. She had no use for the sneers of Voltaire or the atheism of Diderot and so was not an enlightened despot like her son, Joseph II, who managed to alienate practically everybody.

Busy and dedicated as she was as a ruler, Maria Theresa was equally so as a wife and the mother of sixteen children, whose education she supervised diligently. Possibly she was pressed for time when number sixteen came along, because there were still rough edges on Marie Antoinette when she was sent to France as a teenage bride. But that is another story.

Thought and Culture in the Eighteenth Century: The Enlightenment

The so-called Enlightenment was a major development in thought that affected—mostly negatively—the whole intellectual climate of Europe and the Americas. Its impact on politics was perhaps most striking, but it also produced major repercussions in philosophy, economics, art, and many other areas. For religion, its effects were disastrous.

To understand what the Enlightenment actually was, we should recall the character of the Scientific Revolution (discussed in the previous chapter) and how it shaped the seventeenth-century mentality. It was, in fact, the craze for science that produced the Enlightenment. Thinkers seeking a substitute for Catholic truth and traditional philosophy (what Pope Benedict XVI has termed Hellenism) attempted to find the principles of all things in the laws of nature. In his famous little book on the Enlightenment, *The Heavenly City of the Eighteenth-Century Philosophers*, Carl Becker wrote, "Obviously the disciples of the Newtonian philosophy had not ceased to worship. They had only given another form and a new name to the object of worship. Having denatured God, they deified nature.

This deification of nature, which is still a prominent feature of contemporary thought, led the social thinkers of the eighteenth century (known as philosophes—which does not mean philosopher in the traditional sense) to search for natural laws on which to base the whole new world they saw dawning on the horizon. The way in which they went about this project depended on how they viewed nature itself. Some, like Voltaire, saw nature operating according to mathematical laws and concluded that all of society must likewise be ordered "rationally." For this new *rationalism*, clear and abstract principles (which varied according to what each thinker preferred) were to govern all of life. The "irrational" must be strictly excluded, and into this category fell non-abstract, messy things such traditions, customs, and religion. As one thinker put it, "Sitting in my study I can devise laws that can regulate any human society." He didn't need to investigate the *reality* of the conditions for which he was legislating or what people actually wanted; he merely had to come up with what was *rational* in the narrow Enlightenment meaning of that term. Already in the previous century Spinoza had stated, "I shall consider human activities and desires in exactly the same manner as though I were concerned with lines, planes, and solids."

Another way of viewing nature is in terms of immutable physical laws. Newton, after all, had discovered that everything in the physical universe is regulated by laws. He himself certainly did not think this explained all of reality, let alone human affairs, but Newton's discoveries were all the rage in the advanced intellectual circles of the day. ("Nobody understands Newton," Voltaire observed astutely, "but everybody talks about him.") Some of the *philosophes* convinced themselves that all things were so completely determined by inexorable physical laws that free will did not exist—a theory known as *determinism*. Diderot was an exponent of this, at least a few days a week; the other days he was a rationalist—and when his daughter wanted to do something of which he did not approve, he certainly exercised his nonexistent free will, almost as a traditional father would. Determinists and rationalists are rarely consistent. *Determinism* was to have a very long career that has not yet ended. Evolutionism, Marxism, Freudianism, and other systems that find the causes of human affairs in the operation of subhuman or subconscious systems are its children.

A third way of looking at nature is to see the natural world as uncorrupted by civilization. Rousseau, who could be a political rationalist with the best of them, also had a contradictory penchant for exalting sentiment, instinct, and the lack of trammels that he thought characterized "the noble savage." This strain of Enlightenment thought, now known as *Romanticism*, would come into its own a bit later than the other two and would influence nationalism, later trends in the arts, and progressive education—of which Rousseau was one of the originators with his book *Emile*. "When I thus get rid of children's lessons," he wrote, "I get rid of the chief cause of their sorrows, namely their books. Reading is the curse of childhood." In his extremely influential treatise on education—if you can call it that—Rousseau imagines a young boy named Emile brought up on the new principles. He will learn to read only when he has a reason for doing so, such as when he receives a party invitation and does not know what it says. No one will force him, and eventually he will turn out just fine.

We might ask what kind of experience Rousseau had on which to base these startling new theories about child rearing. The answer is: none. He had one position as a private tutor to a couple of children, but he quit when he found that he lost his temper with the children to such an extent that he was afraid of harming them. He also had five children by his mistress, but as they arrived he shuffled them off to an orphanage, where it is presumed they did not long survive. So much for experience.

The point, however, is that the Enlightenment thinker, unlike nearly all earlier thinkers, does not rely on experience to give him his new plans for the world. He merely *thinks*—and produces fine-sounding abstractions. In a *Wall Street Journal* piece entitled "The Heartless Lovers of Mankind," Paul Johnson wrote, "From the time of Voltaire and Rousseau, the secular intellectual has filled the position left by the decline of the cleric, and is proving more arrogant, permanent, and above all more dangerous than his clerical version.... Loving humanity as an idea, they can then produce solutions as ideas. Therein lies the danger ..." as we shall see.

The main characteristics, which are at the same time the evils, of Enlightenment thought are the following: 1) an attitude of *liberalism*, by which the philosophes meant "freedom from" anything they did not like, such as religion ("Crush the infamous thing," thundered Voltaire, referring to the Catholic Church), censorship, restrictions on the economy (they invented laissez-faire), and any other restrictions on human activity disapproved of by the thinker; 2) *idealism*, which would become an important philosophical trend with Kant and his followers, and which privileged ideas over reality; what *is* must be made to conform to the concepts of what *ought to be* as elaborated in the minds of the new thinkers; 3) the glorification of human nature, seen as untainted by Original Sin and requiring only freedom and the removal of societal and religious trammels to become perfect; 4) a utopian view of the future, when Idea will have shaped recalcitrant reality into paradise on earth; 5) atheism or deism, which posits a convenient First Cause that set the universe in motion but shows no real interest in it thereafter and requires nothing from its creatures. The concept of deism is so absurd that I'm inclined to see it as merely a dodge by the philosophes to get their writings past the censors, although I may be wronging them. Possibly some of them actually deluded themselves with this illogicality — most of them were ignorant, after all, of true philosophy. As Father Faber put it, "A deist is only an illogical atheist, and an atheist a logical deist."

Paradoxically, the exaggerated cult of reason and atheism went hand-in-hand with a craze for the occult. In *Fire in the Minds of Men*, James H. Billington discusses this odd phenomenon. Apparently the mind is not really satisfied with rationalism and is fascinated with at least the paranormal, if not the spiritual. Mesmer's hypnotism was all the rage, Benjamin Franklin seems at times to have actually believed in many gods, and we will later find both Marx and Freud dabbling in the occult.

We will observe many consequences of Enlightenment thinking as it affected the ideologies of the nineteenth and twentieth centuries, but here we will concentrate on its philosophical and political premises, with the practical applications deferred until we come to the French and American Revolutions.

To take philosophy first, we may say that idealism, like nominalism, represents a pessimism about the ability of the human mind to know reality—the essences of things. Locke insisted on the validity of sense knowledge, but also claimed that the material substrata of the things perceived by the senses was somehow unknowable. Berkeley, an Anglican bishop, wondered why, in that case, we should say the substratum exists at all. He did away with it, although positing a "spiritual substance" underlying what we perceive. The question also arose of whether things continued to exist if no one perceived them.

These conflicting views were reflected in the following exchange of limericks said to have appeared in a British student publication during the controversy. The first ran,

> There was a young man who said, "God
> Must find it exceedingly odd
> That a sycamore tree simply ceases to be,
> When no one's about on the quad."

The following week someone penned in reply,

> Dear Sir: your astonishment's odd,
> I am always about on the quad.

The Church Under Attack

And that's why the tree continues to be,
Since observed by, Yours Faithfully, God.

Then came Hume, an atheist, who did away with spiritual substance too, being left only with phenomena organized by the mind and based on—apparently—nothing. (He did admit that in practice we must act on the assumption that there is in fact something out there.) Hume's ideas shocked Immanuel Kant; they "woke him from his dogmatic slumbers," as he put it, and he proceeded to pen the dense, difficult, and involved works that have tortured so many generations of philosophy students and caused some Germans to read them in French translation in the hope that they might make more sense that way. For Kant, as for earlier idealists, things in themselves are unknowable and all we perceive is their phenomena. His *Critique of Pure Reason* and *Critique of Practical Reason* became two landmarks of idealist speculative philosophy and ethics and are still enormously influential.

We are here light years away from the sane realism of Aristotle and Aquinas. With idealism replacing realism, there is an abandonment of the object as the focus of attention in favor of the thinking subject. In its extreme form, the preoccupation of idealism and its philosophical descendants with one's own perceptions and thoughts can produce an exaggerated subjectivism that cuts the thinker off from outside reality and even from other people. He is isolated in his own mind, to the point that Jean-Paul Sartre, the twentieth-century existentialist, could say, "Hell is other people"; he also characterized one's reaction to the world as nausea.

On the more practical level, those thinkers who concerned themselves with political and social questions began proposing new schemes and radical reorganizations of society based on the principles of the new thought. While there was considerable variation in the projects they dreamed up, their common watchword was *freedom*. The philosophes attacked many genuine abuses such as slavery and barbaric means of execution of criminals, although they were not by any means the first to do so. Indeed, some of the causes they so loudly espoused as the champions of the downtrodden were already in the process of being eliminated—by the very authorities they despised. Their strident writings and speeches against easy targets, however, made them widely popular with all classes. Their often witty sallies, along with their radical new ideas, were eagerly discussed at the French court, read in pamphlet form, debated in the elegant salons held by prominent Parisian hostesses, and disseminated in the new lodges of the Freemasons.

What were some of the new elements in the thought of these influential circles, which included men such as Thomas Jefferson and Benjamin Franklin in their Paris days? First, there must be new forms of government, developed according to the principles of scientific reasoning rather than being based on custom, tradition, religion, or even past experience. These forms must be in accordance with the new view of human nature as good and perfectible; thus they would accord great freedom to the individual. The individual must have freedom of religion, freedom of speech, and so on. There must be no censorship, no distinctions between classes, no restrictions on the free operation of the "natural laws" that Adam Smith saw regulating the economy.

The first government to be constructed from scratch according to these new principles, produced out of the heads of the new thinkers, was that of the future United States. In *Science and the Founding Fathers*, I. Bernard Cohen demonstrates the influence of the ideas of the Scientific Revolution and the Enlightenment on key American political thinkers such as Jefferson and Franklin. Phrases such as "laws of nature" and "Nature's God" made perfect sense to the deists of the Paris salons, and so did the excoriating of the rule of "tyrants" and the enthusiasm for a great new scientific experiment in government. How its principles were elaborated and why, when the French revolutionaries copied them, they were condemned by the Church is a story for a later episode of this drama.

Chapter 4

Revolutionary Catastrophe

Although the French Revolution began in 1789, its antecedents and inspiration went back much further, and it has never really ended. Every time some discontented rebels decide it would be nice to get out the guns and knives and replace their existing government with something more "democratic," the Revolution is replayed. The very concept—not a Christian one—that revolution is a good thing, the rhetoric all rebels use, and the way they behave when they come out on top are reflections of the great cataclysm of 1789. When we get to the twentieth century we will witness a replay of the Revolution in Russia that bristles with eerie parallels with its French ancestor.

Whenever someone says, "I have a right to ..." more money, abortion, a better job, a satisfying love affair, and so on, he is echoing the revolutionary concept of rights: claims to whatever we happen to desire, regardless of any corresponding obligation or moral context (see the next section). To be fair, not all revolutionaries—not even Mr. Jefferson—would have cared to claim the sordid world we live in as a product of their grand utopian schemes, but abstract principles have a way of leading to unpleasant consequences.

The Church Under Attack

The French Revolution may be said to have begun in earnest on June 17, 1789. In May of that year, at Versailles, King Louis XVI had been persuaded to call a meeting of the Estates General—representatives of the clergy, nobility, and other classes (the Third Estate)—to discuss governmental reforms. He had previously requested input from all over the country as to what changes were necessary to eliminate obsolete practices and exactions that were hindering governmental efficiency. The national debt was large (partly due, ironically, to France's support of the American Revolution), and enemies of the regime made perhaps more of an issue of it than it warranted; it seems to have appeared worse on paper than it was in fact, because of taxes that had not yet been collected. The previous year's weather had been unusually harsh, leading to food shortages during the winter of 1788–1789. The king himself was so dedicated to reform that he had added to the perceived instability of the country by zealously pursuing improvements willy-nilly, often without sufficient follow-through. And he had a great desire to be loved by his people.

Such conditions, however, do not create a revolution. Revolutions are made by men with agendas, and there were plenty of them around. Some, of course, were dead, such as Voltaire, whose recommendation that the Catholic Church be crushed would soon be carried out by his living disciples. The Enlightenment authors who had made daring ideas so fashionable in salons had done their work well; the salons were now political clubs of various stripes, all anxious for a share of power in the new age they hoped to usher in. Some of the shadiest characters were pals of the duke of Orléans, a cousin of King Louis who posed as a liberal and possibly saw himself as a royal replacement for his well-meaning relative.

Revolutionary Catastrophe

And so the Estates met; many of the representatives were no doubt sincere men interested in the common good, but many others were more interested in radical change than in mere re-form. Many nobles balked at the king's tax proposals, while the leaders of the Third Estate, most of them lawyers and many Protestants or Jansenists—hence unfriendly to the Catholic king—demanded a head count instead of the traditional one vote for each estate. The confrontation over this issue led to the formation of a national assembly and a declaration of the sovereignty of "the people" to replace the Estates, on June 17, 1789. The date is significant: June 17 was the day on which, exactly one hundred years earlier, our Lord had revealed to St. Margaret Mary that he wanted the king of France, Louis XIV, to consecrate himself and France to the Sacred Heart. The king refused; his wars and other enterprises went wrong after that, but his successor suffered the ultimate punishment. (There is an ominous reference to this episode in our Lord's words to Sister Lucy of Fatima in August 1931, concerning the papal reluctance to make the consecration to her Immaculate Heart in the man-ner specified: "Make it known to my ministers, given that they follow the example of the King of France in delaying the execu-tion of my request, that they will follow him into misfortune.")

The historical myth of the French Revolution holds that it was good and moderate in the beginning, but somehow went wrong later. The evidence does not support this view. The fol-lowing quotations are from a famous pamphlet called *What Is the Third Estate?* published in the first year of the Revolution by the Abbé Sieyès—a radical priest who supported the Third Estate: "What is the Third Estate? *Everything.* What has it been until now in the political order? *Nothing.* . . . Who is bold enough to maintain that the Third Estate does not contain within itself everything needful to constitute a complete nation? If the privileged order were removed, the nation would not be something less but something more.... Nothing will go well without the Third Estate; everything would go considerably better without the other two.... The nobility may be a *burden* for the nation." (It should be mentioned here that in fact the nobility, the original military defenders of France, were by 1789 a very heterogeneous group, some being desperately poor and others successful middle-class merchants who had bought their titles.)

The ominous implications of the passages quoted above seem obvious. Revolutionaries seek concrete targets at which to direct the energies of the mobs they lead; for Elizabethan Englishmen it was Catholics, and for Marxists it would be the bourgeoisie, but for the Third Estate it was to be the clergy and the nobility. It would not be long before the new revolutionary government would take steps to eliminate the burdensome First and Second Estates with the guillotine.

We cannot follow the progress of the Revolution in detail; it was radical enough at the beginning, when the royal family was taken back to Paris accompanied by mobs waving pikes with severed heads on them, but it grew even more violent with each phase it went through. One by one the royal family died—with the exception of a daughter who was eventually sent to her grandmother's country of Austria as the violence began to peter out. The king was executed first after a series of deliberations, in one of which his cousin the duke of Orléans cast the deciding vote. (The duke's turn soon came. Despite his base attempts to claim that he was really the son of a coachman, the butchers knew an aristocrat when they saw him and decided that his head would look much better removed.) King Louis had impressed on his family while they were together in prison that they must forgive their enemies no matter what, a heroic virtue that they all took to heart. Shortly before his death on January 21, 1793, he made the consecration to the Sacred Heart that our Lord had requested in vain of his ancestor.

The Revolution did not have it all its own way. Following the king's execution, the counterrevolution — a genuine popular movement, in contrast to the elite-orchestrated revolutionary regime — began to organize all over France. The greatest resistance was mounted in the west of France, in the Vendée, where peasants armed with pitchforks persuaded the (sometimes reluctant) nobles of the region to take charge of military organization. In the end they were defeated and gruesomely massacred, but they had shaken the rebel government's control and remained a strong guerilla movement until the end of the revolutionary period. An address by one of their leaders, the Marquis de Charette, illustrates clearly the contrast between the fanatical abstractions of the "enlightened" revolutionaries and Catholic realism:

> For us our country is our villages, our altars, our graves, all that our fathers loved before us. Our country is our Faith, our land, our King. But what is their country? Do you understand? Do you? They have it in their brains; we have it under our feet. It is as old as the devil, the world they call new and would establish in the absence of God. They tell us we are the slaves of ancient superstitions; how ridiculous! But in the face of these demons who are reborn from century to century, we are youth, gentlemen! We are the youth of God, the youth of faithfulness! And this youth intends to preserve, for itself and for its sons, genuine humanity and the liberty of the soul.

The Church Under Attack

Robespierre, with his ideal "republic of virtue" in his brain, decided that terror was the way to achieve it. More and more human obstacles to his utopia perished daily during his Reign of Terror; from March to July 1794, the monthly total of beheadings rose from 122 to 966. Only when the members of the assembly turned against their master, out of fear of being next on his list, did Robespierre make his own trip to the guillotine and revolutionary violence begin to abate. It is interesting to note that Thomas Jefferson, on hearing news of the Reign of Terror, expressed the cold abstraction of the idealist: "My own affections have been deeply wounded by some of the martyrs to this cause, but rather than it should have failed, I would have seen half the earth desolated." A chilling thought, reminiscent of Marx's "What do I care if three-quarters of the earth perish provided the fourth that remains is Communist?"

Queen Marie Antoinette was now left alone with her daughter, since her little son Louis-Charles, now Louis XVII, had been taken from her. Following her trumped-up trial, at which her child was made drunk by his brutal captives and made to repeat filthy charges against her, she was transferred to a solitary cell to await her execution. Her saintly sister-in-law, Madame Elizabeth, who had voluntarily joined the family in prison, remained with her young niece, whom she tried to prepare for the solitary confinement she was soon to endure when her aunt too was taken away. The queen had once, as a very young bride, had a reputation for frivolity and willfulness, despite the constant epistolary advice she received from her mother, the empress Maria Theresa of Austria. She had matured into a courageous and compassionate woman, and her last letter, written at 4:30 a.m. on the date of her execution, October 16, is a moving testament to her nobility of character. It is addressed to Madame

Revolutionary Catastrophe

Elizabeth, to whom the queen entrusted her children, although she had already heard that her daughter and sister-in-law had been separated, and she did not know where her son was.

May my son never forget his father's last words, which I repeat to him now: let him never seek to avenge our death.... I die in the Roman, Catholic, apostolic religion in which I was brought up and which I have always professed, expecting no spiritual consolation, not knowing whether there are still priests of that religion here, but, given where I am, it would no doubt expose them too much if they tried to come here. I sincerely ask forgiveness of God for all the sins that I may have committed in my life.... I ask pardon of all those I have known.... I pardon all my enemies the ill that they have done me.... Farewell, my good and loving sister; may this letter reach you safely! Think always of me, I embrace you with all my heart, as well as my poor, dear children: my God! How dreadful it is to leave them.[5]

In May 1794, Elizabeth was also executed. Her selfless behavior during her imprisonment enhanced her reputation for sanctity, and when her head fell into the basket, there was, contrary to the custom of the mob, no cheering but only silence. Alone in her cell, her niece controlled her anguish and despair in scribbling over and over on the walls, "I forgive them."

Little Louis-Charles lived to the age of ten. After his mother's trial he was alternately neglected and mistreated by his

---

[5] Taken from Last Letters: *Prisons and Prisoners of the French Revolution*, by Olivier Blanc (New York: Farrar, Straus, and Giroux, 1987).

captors, to whom he generally refused to speak—having apparently realized what use they had made of him against his mother. He became extremely ill with what seems to have been a skeletal form of tuberculosis and suffered a great deal. Once he did respond to a mocking question, "What would you do if you were the king and free?" He replied, "I would forgive you." At length he was given a kind jailor, when the Reign of Terror had spent itself, and a doctor, who was able to do nothing for him. On June 8, 1795, he told his jailor that he was still suffering but much less, "because the music is so beautiful." He seemed surprised that the guard asked what music he meant, and he explained that it came from above and that he could hear his mother's voice among the others. A few minutes later, he was dead. His remains were interred in a common grave, but the doctor who performed the autopsy secretly preserved his heart. The relic was preserved by a series of custodians in two or three countries, and finally—duly identified by DNA testing—it was returned to Paris and interred in the royal crypt of the kings of France at St. Denis in June 2004. The ceremony was one of great solemnity, attended by crowds of thousands celebrating the "return of the king."

As for the Revolution, the fanatical Robespierre was replaced in 1794 by a system known as the Directory. That lasted—its members trying to cope with foreign war (France now had all of Europe against her), domestic economic crises, and their own corruption—until a young Corsican general named Napoleon Bonaparte stepped in and simply took control of France in 1799. During those five years popular discontent with the Revolution had been growing, particularly, it seems, among the lower-class women who seem to have supported it originally. Mothers felt keenly the lack of priests to baptize their babies and assist the dying. The very large number of French women who worked as dressmakers, milliners, ladies' maids, and so forth found themselves out of work. Revolutionary puritanism stipulated that only the plainest of dress should be worn by the new citizens of the Republic, so lace-makers and others who engaged in the decorative arts were unwanted and even regarded with suspicion by the culture police. Wealthier women who had employed household help had largely disappeared, and so had the jobs they had provided. The husbands of the increasingly discontented women, meanwhile, spent their time at political clubs and in taking part in mass demonstrations. All this played a role in eroding popular support for the new regime, facilitating the change that was to come in 1799; but that is another story.

Revolutionary Thought and Culture

The turmoil of the eighteenth century, which ran from the outbreak of the American Revolution through the rest of the century, left little opportunity for the flourishing of the Catholic thought and culture we have examined in earlier periods. Certainly there were Catholic thinkers and important work was done; there were saints during this period too, although a good number of them were martyrs of the French Revolution. (St. Alphonsus Ligouri was a very great saint who died two years before the Revolution erupted.)

The great intellectual debate of the period—over whether the Revolution was good or bad and what its basic evils (for conservatives) or benefits (for liberals) were—divides "liberals" and "conservatives" to this day. The famous British critic of the French Revolution, Edmund Burke, wrote while the cataclysm was still unfolding, but other major thinkers who began to study and analyze the nature of revolution did so only in the early nineteenth century, where we will meet them in a later chapter. We can, however, isolate the essential questions raised for Catholics by both the American and French Revolutions: Is revolution ever justified? Is the new ideology of the rights of man compatible with Christian principles?

In traditional thought, revolution against legitimate authority had always been considered a great evil; hence the initial hesitation of the French king to support the American insurgency, even though it was directed at France's main political enemy, Great Britain. Catholic political thinkers, considering the question of overthrowing a ruler, agreed that an illegitimate regime could sometimes be resisted; this is the justification for counterrevolution, whether against the French revolutionaries or against Communist governments. The question of whether a merely harsh, but legitimate, ruler could be opposed with force—the famous tyrannicide issue, much debated in medieval schools—was not so easy to answer, because the evil brought upon the people by armed conflict could be worse than the original oppression. Both traditional Catholic moral principles and concrete circumstances thus shaped European thought on revolution, and in general it was condemned.

With rare exceptions (possibly only Switzerland, because many so-called republics such as Venice were monarchies in disguise) the political model of Christendom from the fifth-century reign of Clovis, the first Catholic king, was monarchy. What its critics would call the accident of birth that brought a ruler to the throne was, to our ancestors, no accident. Obviously God had from all eternity destined each of his children to be born at a certain time and place, and this naturally applied to royalty too. That kings were fallible human beings no one denied, but they were endowed with political *legitimacy* as heirs of their ancestors, and their authority was absolute. Their *authority* was absolute, meaning they were the highest authority in their realm and answered to God for how they governed it, but their actual *power* was generally far more limited than that of the American president. The idea was that the king took care of national defense, the administration of justice, and the rights of the Church—the big stuff—and the people ran their own affairs. (They were not endlessly polled on what they thought of foreign-policy decisions, about which they knew nothing, and made to feel uneasy because they didn't know more.) On this Catholic principle of subsidiarity, the self-government of towns and villages was a real thing. Even during the reign of the seventeenth- and eighteenth-century "absolute" monarchs, many areas of France rarely saw a government official and had far more freedom from government than we do.

American rebels, of course, made out that they were fighting against a "tyrant" (which poor, batty George III certainly was not). It sounded better than their desire to get out of paying the same taxes as the rest of the British Empire. (Someone has calculated that those taxes amounted to what would be in today's money the cost of dinner and a movie.) It was the Americans, too, who first issued a list of "rights" that God was supposed to have bestowed on "all men" who were also "created equal." These rights included not just life, liberty, and the pursuit of happiness, but all those freedoms: of speech, religion, the press, and so forth.

Leaving aside the philosophically questionable propositions such as that human equality and God's endowment of us with rights are self-evident, the Declaration of Independence and the Bill of Rights did introduce new principles into politics that greatly influenced future revolutionaries. French rebels were so impressed that when they came to power one of their first acts was to draw up the Declaration of the Rights of Man and of the Citizen that borrowed extensively from the Declaration of Independence and the American Constitution with its Bill of Rights. (It is worth noting, however, that although the new rights invented by the Enlightenment were supposed to inhere in human nature, they were actually defined by the state.) Catholics raised on such principles are often shocked to learn that Pope Pius VI condemned the Declaration of the Rights of Man and of the Citizen on March 10, 1791, particularly freedom of speech and freedom of religion. Presumably the pope had not condemned the American prototypes of the French document because the United States was a Protestant country unlikely to listen to the Vicar of Christ, whereas France was the eldest daughter of the Church. On what grounds, though, would any pope condemn principles that we have all been taught are good?

Here we come to a most important difference between the Catholic idea of rights and that of the atheist/deist/Masonic revolutionaries of the eighteenth century. I must observe here that the subject is a broad one requiring numerous distinctions. It took me twenty-two pages and forty-two footnotes to discuss it in another publication some years ago. Hence what follows is necessarily sketchy and includes only a few points. Catholic thought had always included the concept of rights, usually called "liberties" in early documents, but that concept was neither abstract nor detached from concrete circumstances. Rights were considered as counterparts of duties; when the duty ceased to exist, so did the right. A parent, for example, has a duty to educate his child and therefore the right to do so—no matter what the state may say about it. When the child is grown, or if he dies, both the parental duty and the right also cease to exist. Similarly, a man has a duty to support his family and therefore has a right to do so. In an extreme case in which a family was starving, the father would have a moral right to steal in order to fulfill his God-given duty.

What the pope objected to in the French manifesto was the idea of universal and abstract rights unconnected to either obligation or societal context. There *is* no free-speech right to speak blasphemy, for example, because there can be no possible obligation to do so. There is no right for a publisher to publish pornography, because there can be no conceivable duty to do so. Likewise, there is no "inalienable" right to profess a false religion; those in error can be tolerated out of charity and societal concerns, but since they can have no obligation to lead others into error, they have no right to proselytize. To some readers this view of rights may be novel and even disturbing; it was, however, part of the fabric of Catholic society until the Enlightenment and the Revolution began to undermine it. On a practical level, we can look at the operation of the "rights" ideology in our own society. We profess freedom of speech and freedom of the press, and the result is that we are drowning in a sea of blasphemy and pornography and are unable to turn off the tap. There are simply no principles within our political ideology that allow us to cope effectively with our obscene culture or suppress even the craziest of sects. And of course once the rights ideology—now, perhaps, the *religion* of rights—is established, it spawns ever-new rights: the rights of perverts, the rights of the child, the right to homosexual unions, the right to die. None of these was born from a Catholic sense of duty, but neither were their ancestors in Mr. Jefferson's head. The words of the Marquis de Charette quoted earlier express well the distinctions between Catholic realism and Enlightenment idealism, with their somber conclusion: "It is as old as the devil, the world they call new and would establish in the absence of God." The whole course of the revolution, and indeed of all of history, is a playing out of the principles — true or false — rooted in men's minds, hearts, and souls. This is why ideas matter.

Not all the new ideas of the eighteenth century were bad. The most "revolutionary" developments in education, for example, were pioneered by the Catholic Church. By the outbreak of the French Revolution, the Christian Brothers founded by St. John Baptist de la Salle had been educating French boys for over a hundred years. (There were also schools for girls run by other orders.) St. John had died in 1719, but his work had flourished. The Brothers provided free basic education, thoroughly imbued with Catholic doctrine and formation, for the poor in numerous French towns and cities. They led sacrificial lives, rising very early to perform their spiritual exercises, teaching large classes of students all day, and correcting endless papers. They realized that the traditional classical curriculum was not suitable or necessary for all their pupils, so they created innovative programs: while boys destined for university could take the classical curriculum, those aiming at a career in business would take the business course. There were also courses in the latest scientific developments. In fact, the Brothers were far more radical than Voltaire, who seemed to have had no use for the common people and thought it best to keep them in ignorance; the Brothers, on the contrary, wanted to "enlighten" them in the true sense. Even the revolutionaries did not immediately act against the Christian Brothers, while suppressing other religious orders, because of the obvious good they were doing. The Civil Constitution of the Clergy of 1790, however, made the clergy employees of the state, elected by the people, and required to take an oath to the state, which they could not in conscience do. Thirty of the thirty-four French bishops, and 90 percent of the clergy as a whole, refused. This marked them as enemies of the people, to be hunted down and killed.

One of the Christian Brothers caught up in the maelstrom of the Revolution was Brother Solomon, a middle-aged teacher who was temporarily in Paris when the September Massacres broke out in 1792 and was unable to leave. From his letters, fascinating details of life in the capital for a man in hiding have emerged. He dressed as a layman and lived in an apartment, but he did not know how to cook; a kindly housewife who took pity on him taught him a few simple recipes. Two weeks before the events that were to claim his life, Brother Solomon wrote to his family, "Why should we weep, since the Gospel tells us to rejoice when we have something to endure for the name of Christ?... It would seem that I am not worthy to suffer for Him, since I have not as yet endured any trials, whereas so many confessors of the Faith are in affliction." He was soon to join them.

The details of the September Massacres, which took more than a thousand lives, are known from the accounts of eyewitnesses who escaped; thus we have a description of an incident on September 2 in which carriages transporting prisoners were stopped and the prisoners slaughtered. The mob seized Abbé Sicard, one of the priests who had pioneered the teaching of the deaf and dumb. As a sword hovered above his head, a watchmaker named Monnot threw himself in front of the priest, crying, "Kill me rather than sacrifice a man so useful to his country!" The butchers were temporarily taken aback and the abbé pushed out of the way. Later a search was made for him, but he was not recognized and his enemies decided he must have been killed after all. (He survived and lived until 1822.)

As for Brother Solomon, he was arrested on August 15, 1792, and was asked if he had taken the oath to the constitution. When he admitted he had not, he was taken to the prison set up in the former Carmelite seminary, where many clergy of all ranks were confined. On the day that saw Abbé Sicard spared, the howling mob was allowed into the seminary, where the prisoners were taking their exercise. Many were horribly butchered before one of the officers ordered the remaining prisoners inside. There they were again questioned about the oath, and after answering they were sent back to the garden. They went quietly, praying or reading the Divine Office. As they descended into the garden, murderers on either side of the staircase butchered them one by one.

The place remains as it was then. Once a week a scholarly priest gives a tour of the seminary, the tombs of the martyrs, and the little museum with its pathetic exhibits connected with the many prisoners who passed through in the course of the Revolution. The only memorial of those who died in the garden is an inscription on the stone support of the little staircase: Hic Ceciderunt—"Here they fell."

The story of the Carmelites of Compiègne, who survived the early persecutions but finally perished on July 17, 1794, is well known from the memoir of the one sister who was away from her community on an errand and thus survived. Gertrude von Le Fort, Georges Bernanos, and opera composer Poulenc all produced works drawn from the memoir, but the truth is more gripping than any fiction. The women had for many months consecrated themselves daily in preparation for the day when they might become victims, and their steadfastness and courage impressed even their executioners. When they were accused of being fanatics and counterrevolutionaries, Mother Henriette de Jesus asked for a definition of the terms. Hearing that they meant "attachment to your religion and the King," she then bade her sister to rejoice, for they would have the joy of dying for the Faith. They went one by one to the guillotine, chanting joyously, with the mother prioress encouraging each one until all the voices but hers were still.

Chapter 5

Napoleon and After

Napoleon's takeover of France in 1799 went surprisingly smoothly. As a successful general he was popular with many in the government, who mistakenly saw him as a useful tool. His rise to power involved securing the approval or acquiescence of key political figures and was not without its lighter side. One of his speeches before the Council of Five Hundred was not well received, which of course irritated him. As the agitation continued, his brother Lucien, one of many relatives he would use to maintain power, brought in troops to clear the chamber. The council members found it a bit hard to clear out fast, since — as self-styled heirs of the Roman Republic — they were wearing togas (red, for some reason). When you're speeding toward the nearest exit in a panic and a toga, the odds are against getting very far without tripping. (This cult of ancient forms of government, common to both the new United States and revolutionary France, is revealing. Intellectual politicians in both countries, when looking for a model for their new utopias, deliberately passed over the Catholic politics of the medieval period, so rich in political philosophy and sane principles, and ended up with systems that had actually failed in the ancient world.) And of course even togas could not prevent the collapse of the Directory in the face of the charismatic and ruthless Bonaparte. After that it was a piece of cake for Napoleon. Remarking that "constitutions should be short and obscure," he wrote a new one for France. In theory, "the people" were sovereign and there was a three-man executive; in practice, Napoleon controlled everything from the army to administration and diplomacy to proposing all laws. It was hard to recognize the Jacobin he had formerly been in the dictator whose new goal was the restoration of order in France.

What had Napoleon been doing before becoming head of state? Mostly he had been involved in the victorious French campaigns against the rest of Europe. He had also been busy kidnapping the pope. This was Pius VI, the eighty-year-old pontiff who had been reigning for twenty-five years—the longest reign since St. Peter's. When Bonaparte arrived in Italy in 1796, he found that Pius was unwilling to turn over the Papal States to a revolutionary general. The pope was ordered to leave Rome and hounded from town to town until he was finally taken as a captive to France. There he was moved around some more, although he was not only old but ill, and finally died saying, "Father, forgive them." Bonaparte referred to him exultantly as "Pius the last." Meanwhile Napoleon's brother Joseph was put in charge of Italy.

Two years later Bonaparte was in Egypt to cut Great Britain's connection with India. In 1798, in the course of this expedition, he took over Malta, then still under the rule of the Knights. Since their rule forbade taking up arms against fellow Christians (although Bonaparte's qualifications for that title were pretty meager), the Knights ended up going into what turned out to be permanent exile. While in Egypt, the visionary

Napoleon and After

Napoleon talked of building a canal at Suez and brought along a scholar named Champollion, the first to decipher Egyptian writing by means of the Rosetta Stone. Napoleon lost the Battle of Nile to Nelson and the British fleet, fought with the Ottoman Turks, and then cut short what he called the "romantic interlude" to beetle back to Paris in time to foil the plans of his political enemies. From 1798 to 1801 the War of the Second Coalition (made up of Great Britain, Austria, and Russia) raged. France was now both scared and anxious for a competent leader to deal with the crisis. This is where Bonaparte made his bid for power, in the beginning as "first consul," a Roman title that sounded better than "dictator." He made a concordat with the papacy, since the dead Pius had not been the last after all and there was now a Pius VII. According to the concordat, the French master got what he wanted. The Church accepted the loss of her lands, Napoleon was allowed to *nominate* bishops, whom the pope would *appoint*, and Catholicism was no longer the religion of France but only "of the majority of Frenchmen."

Domestically, Napoleon provided France with a new law code and its first central bank. He centralized control of the country as no absolute king had ever done, wiping out what little local self-government had survived the Revolution. Victorious France was now briefly at peace, surrounded by a gaggle of puppet states in Holland, Italy, and Switzerland. Bonaparte also had plans for a great colonial empire, partly based on Louisiana and Haiti (a stopover for ships en route to America). Haiti's slave population, however, had revolted during the French Revolution and had come under the charismatic leadership of the Catholic Toussaint l'Ouverture. The French government, which took a dim view of other people's revolutions, attempted to suppress the revolt, capturing Toussaint and imprisoning him in a cold French prison until he died. Haitian resistance continued, however, and not even Napoleon's forces were a match, in the end, for yellow fever and guerilla warfare. Bonaparte was forced to unload Louisiana on Thomas Jefferson for the bargain price of $11 million. Napoleon had no authority to sell off a French possession, and Jefferson had no congressional authority to purchase it, but they did it anyway in 1803.

The saga of Napoleon Bonaparte still had eleven years to run—of course, he thought it would be more, and to many it must have felt like a lot more—and he decided it was about time to become an emperor instead of merely a first consul. The vote he held in 1804 came out 3,600,000 for an empire and 2,600 against. (This is the sort of thing that drives liberals crazy—you give the common man the vote, and he elects an emperor.) For his coronation, Napoleon had Pope Pius VII brought to Paris. The pope seems to have been used merely as window dressing because—in a do-it-yourself mood—Napoleon took the crowns from his hands and proceeded to crown both himself and his wife, Josephine (whom he would later divorce when she failed to produce an heir).

The self-made emperor was soon embroiled in the War of the Third Coalition (Austria, Russia, Sweden, and later Prussia). He blockaded Great Britain, which he called "a nation of shopkeepers" that would be hurt most by lack of imports and exports. (The blockade hurt France too, though, and the English smuggled British goods into the continent labeled "Made in France.") The plan was for the emperor to invade Great Britain once it was softened up by the blockade, but his invasion never got off the ground. The French fleet had been ordered to sail directly from the West Indies to the English Channel, but it made a stop at a Spanish port, where Admiral Nelson located it, and the famous Battle of Trafalgar took place in 1805. It was a great British victory: Nelson destroyed half the French ships and lost not one of his own, although he did lose his life.

So much for the fleet. The French army was intact, though, and after their victory over the Allies at Austerlitz William Pitt sighed, "Roll up the map of Europe; we won't need it for another ten years." Perhaps imitating Julius Caesar's division of Gaul into three parts, Napoleon divided Europe similarly into: the French Empire, composed of France and adjacent territories such as Belgium; the satellites, mostly ruled by his relatives; and the defeated states he had forced into alliance with France. These included Austria, Prussia, and Russia. Only Great Britain, Sweden, and the Ottoman Empire were outside the system, and of these only Great Britain counted for anything as an adversary. By 1806 France was supreme on the continent; Napoleon took over large chunks of Austria and Prussia, reducing them to second-rate powers, and the following year he tinkered with the map of Europe some more.

This tinkering, however, was beginning to get on the nerves of his millions of victims, and resentment and nationalist sentiment began to take shape all over Europe. The Napoleonic army had been spectacularly successful, but its tactics were carefully noted and later imitated by those it conquered, with ominous results for the French. Two adventures in particular were to shake the morale of the military and lead to the emperor's downfall.

The first was the war in Spain. Napoleon had plunked his brother Joseph down on the Spanish throne in 1808, apparently thinking that meant the country was his. One anti-Spanish college textbook refers to this relative as "gentle brother Joseph"—as if the barbaric Spaniards had no business revolting against such a sweet and benevolent man. The Spanish didn't see it that way and began a guerilla war that would last for years and cost up to a hundred French lives each day, with a total of as many as three hundred thousand. At first the emperor did not believe his gentle brother's statements as to the need for hundreds of thousands of troops (and also a hundred thousand gallows), but he was finally persuaded to march into Spain and enter Madrid in December 1808. French invincibility was on the wane, however, as two incidents in that year demonstrate.

The first was the heroic resistance of the town of Zaragoza to a siege by the French that went on for months. The whole population was involved in the defense, with women manning guns and citizens digging tunnels to meet the ones the French were digging under the walls. Glass and nails became the defenders' ammunition when bullets ran out, and capitulation was steadily refused. When the survivors finally surrendered, French morale was greatly shaken by the sight of what a ragged little band had foiled the Grande Armée for so long. Meanwhile the Duke of Wellington had landed in Portugal with a relatively small force; they were as persistent as the Zaragozans, however, and did not quit until they entered France six years later.

Elsewhere in Europe, resistance grew. Farmers in the Tyrol took up pitchforks and followed the innkeeper Andreas Hofer in fighting the French. The Italians put up crosses to replace the French "trees of liberty." Napoleon would soon teach them a lesson, though; he would take over the Papal States and kidnap that pope who should never have been elected. Pius VII absolutely refused to capitulate to French demands and was hauled around from prison to prison in Italy and France, often in harsh conditions, during a five-year captivity. Showing no resentment, he urged leniency for his tormentor when he ultimately fell and welcomed exiled members of the erstwhile imperial family to Rome with kindness.

Meanwhile what was to prove his downfall was emerging in Napoleon's busy brain as a brilliant scheme: he would invade Russia in 1812. Perhaps the largest army in history—around six hundred thousand men—entered Russia in late June. Led ever further into the country by the retreating Russian army, then caught by the Russian winter, the French army that staggered out of Russia in December included only a few thousand men. Undeterred by the massive loss of human life, Bonaparte immediately raised—incredibly—another army of four hundred thousand. He could not as readily replace lost equipment, however, and the Battle of the Nations (Leipzig) in 1813 drove him back into France and compelled him to abdicate and accept exile on the Mediterranean island of Elba. End of Napoleon, right?

So Europe thought. The Congress of Vienna began its leisurely restoration of prerevolutionary Europe in September 1814, approving the accession of the brother of the late King Louis XVI (and uncle of the little King Louis XVII) to the French throne as Louis XVIII. The delegates were still restoring peace and order, combining it with not a little socializing at parties and balls, in February 1815. That was when the Austrian Minister Metternich, the council's leader, went to bed very late one night and put off reading the message he saw on his table. In the morning he was horrified to learn that it was from the British commander in the Mediterranean asking if anyone had seen Napoleon Bonaparte.

The emperor had done it again. With his sisters' jewels, ships had been procured to take him from Elba to France, and he was about to march to Paris. The Congress of Vienna hastily became a council of war, while Louis XVIII sent troops to arrest Napoleon. They were led by Marshal Ney, who boasted that he would bring the upstart back in a cage. Meanwhile Bonaparte's march (along what is now known to tourists and fans of Napoleon as "Napoleon's Route") became a triumphal procession, with crowds cheering, "Long live the emperor!" and only a few discordant notes of "Long live the king!" And this for a man responsible for the deaths of hundreds of thousands of his own people. No French troops would fire on him, and when Ney arrived and came face-to-face with his old commander, he broke a tense silence with "Long live the emperor!" and joined him once again.

Only in the sane and Catholic west of France—the Vendée—did the people resist the demagogue and revolt for "Church and Crown." Napoleon was forced to send ten thousand troops to deal with this rebellion, which he would sorely miss in his last great gamble: the Battle of Waterloo, on June 18, 1815. Napoleon seemed strangely unlike himself during this fateful battle, possibly due to illness. The timing of some of his commands to various troop units was off, and he seems to have wasted valuable time in not following up advantages. Still, the British were hard pressed. The Prussians, under Field Marshal Blücher, were to join the British, under Wellington, at Waterloo but were delayed by a defeat they had suffered two days earlier. Blücher, aged 72, had been trapped under his fallen horse and badly shaken up; nevertheless, he managed to remount and set off for Waterloo, where an exhausted Wellington was saying, as the day was drawing to a close, "Night or the Prussians must come." The Prussians did come, and soon it was all over for Napoleon. Distrusting his own people, he fled to the coast, where he surrendered to the commander of a British ship. He was exiled this time to a remote south Atlantic island—St. Helena—from which only death would deliver him. He seems to have died reconciled to the Church.

The Congress of Vienna, under the guidance of Metternich, went back to restoring boundaries and maintaining the peace of Europe; it also had the sense to treat France leniently and allow it to rejoin the family of nations after demonstrating stability and paying an indemnity. As for French politics, the monarchy was restored, although with a difference. Louis XVIII granted a charter setting up a constitutional monarchy and a chamber of deputies, which institutionalized partisan squabbling and provided a means for leftover revolutionaries and others to undermine the regime. Under Charles X, brother of Louis XVI and Louis XVIII, another revolution broke out; thereafter they occurred at intervals, like earthquakes, until after World War II, and few historians would bet that there will not be another one. We will look at these issues in a subsequent chapter.

Thought and Culture in the Early Nineteenth Century

The French Revolution and the Napoleonic era embodied principles that were often anti-Catholic and contrary to the traditions of Western civilization, and this was obvious to men of discernment at the time. It was not until the dust had settled, however, and a new century was well underway that the many consequences, both immediate and long-term, of those principles came into clear focus.

Albert Guérard, a cultural historian, has summarized French cultural history from the sixteenth through the eighteenth century in this way: "We find at first Reason working in cheerful subordination to Tradition; then Reason emancipated, but still respectful; Reason defiant; Reason triumphant. Some would be tempted to add: Reason … going mad on its accession to power." We have already seen something of how the "reason" so dear to Enlightenment thinkers became the source of previously unthinkable atrocities.

The material consequences of the revolutionary and Napoleonic eras were bad enough: two million Frenchmen were dead, which equals the combined totals for World War I and World War II, and this does not include the rest of Europe. The Revolution directly executed some four hundred thousand people, of whom only some ten percent were those nobles who were its ostensible targets. In politics, Alexis de Tocqueville pointed out that the Revolution took over centralized government and made it despotic: wiping out classes, traditions, vested interests, which had previously stood as buffers between the individual and the state. Before the Revolution, we might say, the king was at the top of the pyramid and a peasant named Jacques was at the bottom. Between them there were many organisms: Jacques' village, parish, guild, cooperative, provincial government, diocese, and so forth. The king was responsible for the peace of the realm, public order, and defense. Jacques had a say in the doings of those intermediary bodies that most nearly concerned him.

After the Revolution, we find a centralized government and power structure at the top and Jacques still at the bottom while in between them is … almost nothing. The old traditional buffers are gone, and Jacques is at the mercy of the central government with its universal military service (an invention of the Revolution); all-seeing tax collectors; standardized, compulsory education in state schools; and so on. Later in the century, a minister of education would boast that if you told him the age of a French child, he could tell you exactly what that child was doing at that moment, so regimented were the French state schools. Of course, some things were done that everyone agreed were good; usually they were things that the king had wanted in the first place, such as the abolition of some outmoded fees and taxes and some equalizing of the tax burden.

In the short term, as with the Reformation, the upheaval in social services was catastrophic. We have only to think of the suppression of the religious orders and the collapse of their work of education, nursing, care of the sick and the indigent, and so forth.

No family was untouched. Imagine Jacques, happy at the idea of tax relief when the Revolution began, but horrified at the persecution of the Church and the murder of the royal family; perhaps he helped to hide hunted priests, and perhaps they were discovered and butchered; he would also have had to hide his wife and daughters from the rampaging mobs and see his sons taken by the military draft—many such sons would never return or would come home maimed. When, finally, all was relatively calm again, the politicians could say to Jacques, "You're free, citizen! You've got liberty, equality, and fraternity. Wasn't it worth it?" There were millions of Jacques, who all paid the price of the Revolution, and only some thought it was worth it.

This split in French society, and indeed throughout the world, between those who think the French Revolution was a good thing and those who think it was a bad thing endures even today and divides liberals from conservatives. The words *liberty, equality, fraternity* would be much used in the nineteenth and twentieth centuries, with varying shades of meaning. Equality would become a substitute for religion in Marxism, for example. Fraternity would reinforce nationalism, socialist "brotherhoods," and other new isms we will encounter later. Liberty, which sounds so good, with its "rights of man" ideology, was analyzed earlier in this book.

Early nineteenth-century liberals, then, were generally those who admired the principles of the French Revolution, sharing its exasperation with religion and tradition and its insistence on "liberty." They also espoused the free-market economics now associated with "conservatives," and in their early days they were antidemocratic. The "liberty" they preached was for educated folk like themselves; they did not necessarily want either to educate the common man or to give him the vote. It was only later that they became "democrats," although their elitism continued to pop up at odd times. Someone complained to a mid-nineteenth-century liberal French government minister that he was unable to vote because he did not meet the property requirement that was then a condition of voting. The minister's advice was: "Just get rich." This limitation of suffrage to the rich made sense, of course, given the tendency of the masses to vote for emperors instead of businessmen. Kings and emperors were likely to get in the way of the rich and liberal bourgeoisie running the country, so the answer was to restrict the vote to well-off voters disinclined to rock the political boat. (How many leading liberals can you count today who are not rich?)

As for laissez-faire capitalism, liberals began to shift ground on that later in the nineteenth century, partly because of the obvious evils of unhampered industrialization and partly because of the new attractions of socialist ideology. Now they were no longer cheering for Adam Smith but for social reforms of all kinds and even for a scruffy man with a beard and a German accent who thought the class struggle was the key to understanding all things.

Napoleon and After

Whatever the contradictions between theory and practice in their lives, nineteenth-century liberals in general continued to profess the Enlightenment ideas we have already considered. Various factions within liberalism included diehards determined to fight the French Revolution all over again and make it come out right this time, comfortable bourgeois businessmen, and wishy-washy monarchists who wanted a parliamentary system with a figurehead monarch like the British. There were various subspecies within all these categories, and there was also a growing population of exploited workers who tended to make liberals nervous; even during the French Revolution the suggestion that economic equality would be nice led to savage suppression of the suggesters.

On the other hand, there was conservatism. Politically, this was embodied in the restoration of monarchy and the policies of the Congress of Vienna, such as the agreement to stamp out revolution whenever it should reemerge in Europe. This represents the reemergence of the idea of order as the highest political good: "Order is very precious to the common man," someone—probably Chesterton, who uttered so many ready-made quotations—has said.

The Congress, and Prince Metternich in particular, used to be much blamed for thus repressing the "rights" and "self-determination of peoples." Following the ghastly bloodbaths of the twentieth century, however, political thinkers such as Henry Kissinger noticed that Metternich's policies had actually kept the general peace of Europe for a hundred years—from 1815 to the outbreak of World War I. While there were indeed many revolutions during that period, and conflicts such as the Franco-Prussian War, there was no war that involved the whole continent as there had been in the centuries before and after the nineteenth century—quite an achievement for Metternich's "Congress Diplomacy."

The political achievement of conservatism, which was seen as preserving public order and the valuable contributions of the past, was only one facet of the vigorous development of the conservative mentality in the nineteenth century. Some manifestations of conservatism were, ironically, influenced by a cultural movement that owed much to the philosophe Rousseau. This was Romanticism, a reaction against the extreme rationalism of the eighteenth century. Romanticism emphasized sentiment and emotion, rather than abstract reasoning, and greatly influenced the literature, art, and music of the period. It also reinforced the conservative attachment to the Catholic past, particularly the previously despised Middle Ages. This new interest resulted in the emergence for the first time of scholarly medieval studies, with emphasis on the collection and analysis of source material. Modern scientific history, of both the Church and various Christian nations, made great strides due to this new interest in conserving the heritage of the past. After the iconoclasm of the French Revolution, in which priceless Catholic artistic treasures were lost forever, the rediscovery of the Catholic past in all countries was a heartening development.

To summarize the differences in outlook between conservatism and liberalism, which remain to the present, although true conservatism has long been dying a slow death, we may consider these points:

- *Philosophical approach*: for liberals it is idealism: they operate according to utopian schemes they evolve within their heads since they accept no fixed and natural social order. Examples: feminism, homosexual

"rights," socialism, and so forth. For conservat.
the other hand, the philosophical framework is realism, with its insistence on an objective and knowable
moral and social order.

- *Human nature*: for liberals it is perfectible; for conservatives it is flawed (earlier we considered the consequences of these two views).

- *Law*: for liberals it is the expression of the common
  will; for conservatives it is the expression of God's law
  and objective order.

- *Society*: for liberals it is composed of individual human
  atoms; for conservatives it is communitarian — made
  up of all those "bodies" dear to corporatism: family,
  Church, guild, and so on.

- *Political ideal*: for liberals it is liberty; for conservatives,
  order and the common good.

- *Rights*: for liberals rights are the claims or wants of
  individuals, defined by the state and changeable; for
  conservatives they are the counterpart of man's duties
  toward God and others and are independent of what
  a state might decree.

It is obvious that no real compromise is possible between
these opposing views of human nature and society and that
policies stemming from them will differ radically. From 1815 to
1830 conservatism was largely triumphant in politics and culture. It began to weaken throughout the rest of the century, under the onslaughts of both a tenacious "old" liberalism and the
"new" liberalism of socialism and other isms. We will observe

the melancholy progress of this development, and the popes and saints caught up in it, in a subsequent chapter. The political developments and new ideologies of the nineteenth century, in fact, would be among the greatest challenges that Christendom has ever faced.

Chapter 6

The Mid-Nineteenth Century

Here comes another one of those overly busy periods in history to which no mere chapter can do justice. There is too much going on in every area: revolutions go off like firecrackers all over the place, politics careens from the establishment of radical revolutionary regimes to the emergence of brand new monarchies, and we have to consider many developments in nineteenth-century science, technology, and social thought because they continue to have repercussions today. We will do what we can to make sense of it all—or at least some of it.

We begin with France again. The eldest daughter of the Church, her Faith now partially undermined by liberalism, remained for most of the nineteenth century the bellwether of Europe in many ways. In 1830, a revolution broke out in Paris against King Charles X, brother of Louis XVI. It occurred during particularly nice July weather, since it is always easier for revolutionaries to get people out on the streets yelling if the weather is good. Objections to the king's rule were largely trivial. He had appointed members of the religious teaching orders to positions in state schools. This made eminent sense because they were experts in teaching and had, in fact, created the modern

French educational system. Liberals who wanted the schools to be centers of indoctrination in their own ideology were angry. They also did not like the king's plan for compensating victims of the Revolution for the loss of their property. The plan was financed by lowering the interest on government bonds by two percentage points, which also irritated middle-class investors. The radicals, who dearly wanted to replay the French Revolution, less extreme liberals, and the wealthy bourgeoisie were all represented in the growing opposition to Charles, while the liberal press incited the malcontents of Paris to take to the streets, which they gladly did.

The situation then turned ugly. Nuns and priests were beaten and killed, and the city hall was occupied; there were students and workers demanding the revolutionary republic of 1795, the bourgeoisie and bankers favoring a constitutional monarchy, and the liberals within the parliament desiring something like what England got after the so-called "Glorious Revolution" of 1688. Armed conflict was imminent when the Marquis de Lafayette, now a venerable figure respected by all leftist factions, stepped in and calmed the situation. The result was the accession of Louis-Philippe, duke of Orléans, as king of France. His father had been the wretch "Philippe Egalité," who had helped foment the original French Revolution but ended up guillotined. The son professed the ideas of Voltaire and Rousseau, but was not an extremist. He dressed and acted like a sober, wealthy businessman who admired republicanism. So King Charles fled to England, the flag was changed from that of the royal family to the revolutionary tricolor, and the bourgeoisie triumphed with a man after their own grasping hearts. He was called the Citizen King, an odd combination of terms evoking both the Terror and the traditional monarchy. He also had the misfortune to be pear-shaped, which gave endless scope to the political cartoonists of the day.

News of the revolution in France spread across Europe and sparked imitations, although often with quite different motivations from those that had stirred up the French. Next door in Belgium, the Catholic population had been seething beneath the rule of the Protestant Dutch, under which the Congress of Vienna, in one of its few glaring blunders, had placed them. Obtuse (and obstinate) King William had refused to grant the traditional privileges of the Church, allowed the Belgians only a fraction of the legislative seats to which the size of their population entitled them, and generally oppressed and exasperated his southern subjects. It seems that in August 1830 many Belgian citizens, brooding over their wrongs, attended a performance in Brussels of an opera about a revolution in Naples. Why, they must have asked each other during the intermission, can't we do what they did in Paris last month and get rid of this dolt William with a revolution like the one we saw on stage? No sooner thought than done. They poured out into the streets and soon had themselves a king of the Belgians: Leopold I, of German origin. His regime was a constitutional monarchy with provision for much local self-government. The Congress of Vienna powers met to discuss this breach in their arrangements and decided to guarantee Belgian independence. King William, however, refused to get the message. Not once but twice, in 1831 and 1832, he came tramping into Belgium with his army, trying to reconquer the place. Britain and France defeated him both times, and finally he subsided.

Catholic Poland in 1830 was under the benign rule of Russian Czar Alexander I, who in 1815 had granted the most liberal constitution in Europe. (Russia itself had had its Decembrist

The Church Under Attack

Revolt in 1825, which had been suppressed.) The Poles had a great deal of self-government and control of their own administration and army. When Alexander's more conservative brother Nicholas came to the throne in 1825, impractical Polish nationalists began insisting not only on strict observance of the constitution but also on the restoration of vast tracts of Russian territory that had belonged to Poland in earlier ages. The fever of exalted nationalism was cultivated within secret societies within the army, although their members lacked the support of the Polish people. The uprising they provoked and the consequent Russian military intervention coincided with the first outbreak of cholera in Europe, causing great suffering and misery. And it was all for nothing: Nicholas had restored order by 1833 and also closed the Polish universities because they had been a source of revolutionary ideas. The young liberal intellectuals fled the country, as we will see them doing in other countries when their utopian revolts fail. In often-comfortable exile, they dramatized themselves as noble, romantic heroes, leaving the common people at home to face the sad consequences of their idealism.

There were outbreaks of revolutionary agitation in other states of Europe also, but we will have to catch up with them later on and return to France now, lest we miss the next — more spectacular — blowup. Back in Paris, then, the bourgeois regime of the Citizen King presided over the stepped-up economic activity brought about by the ongoing Industrial Revolution. Tocqueville wrote, "Government in those days resembled an industrial company whose every operation is undertaken for the profits which the stockholders may gain thereby." The stockholders were the mere two hundred thousand qualified voters (investors, businessmen, and so forth). The misery and dislocation caused by rapid industrialization was of little concern to them.

By 1848, a number of varieties of opposition to the government had surfaced: those who wanted a constitutional monarchy; the old republicans who still harked back wistfully to the original Revolution; socialists, who gained support during the economic depression of the 1840s; and, strangely enough, Bonapartists. The latter were characterized by a rather vague nostalgia stimulated by the return of Napoleon's remains from Elba to Paris in 1840—the legendary glamour of the great emperor contrasted sharply with the stodginess of their unglamorous, peace-loving, pear-shaped king.

One of the most significant of modern revolutions began in February 1848 with a political dispute over the office of chief minister, combined with the holding of political banquets in various parts of Paris. One of these turned into a huge demonstration, which soon became a riot; troops fired on the crowd, and the government collapsed into crisis. Perhaps there is not much backbone to a pear, because the king abdicated almost immediately and a provisional government took over, setting up national workshops for the unemployed and calling the first elections in European history in which almost the whole male population voted. They chose nine hundred middle-class moderate deputies, with only a sprinkling of radicals, and it looked as if the transfer of power had been successful. Unfortunately, the radicals refused to quit, stirring up a mob to invade the assembly, which closed the government workshops in retaliation.

This triggered the "June Days": the first large-scale outbreak of class warfare in modern European history. (Karl Marx was there, as we will see later on. He did not take part in the fighting, however; he was not that kind of Communist.) The prospect of social revolution spread panic and called forth strong repression under the command of General Cavaignac; fifteen hundred were killed and four thousand deported to places like Algeria.

Then we have the very interesting results of the December elections. Out of seven million votes, Cavaignac got one and a half million and the Republicans got half a million. But five million votes went to the winner, Louis-Napoleon Bonaparte. The common man had done it again—give him the vote, and he elects a Bonaparte or an emperor, which is what Louis-Napoleon—nephew of the original—would soon become. He started as mere head of the new republic, but a coup d'état on December 2, 1851, the date of the coronation of Napoleon I, would change that. The vote he held then, on his authority to draw up a new constitution, was 7,500,000 in favor and only half a million opposed. By December 2, 1852, he was Emperor Napoleon III (the third, because the first Napoleon's son had died young). He was emperor of the masses, he said, updating the Napoleonic approach to politics, and he would be a reformer too. Like the first French Revolution, the Revolution of 1848 had produced first a republic and then a Napoleonic empire. Bonaparte III would reign until 1870, but although he tried repeatedly to emulate his unrepeatable uncle, he just couldn't manage the military glory business and most of his adventures turned sour. We will come back to him.

Meanwhile 1848 had become a year of revolutions all across Europe, with the epidemic of violence affecting most countries. There was a revolt in Vienna in March, which caused Metternich to flee. He too went to England, which seems to have been pretty well stuffed with toppled rulers and politicians by the century's end. Soon revolutions broke out in Prague and

The Mid-Nineteenth Century

Hungary. The young firebrand Lajos Kossuth led an all-out war for Hungarian independence from Austria, while minorities within Hungary declared their independence from everybody. The republic declared by Kossuth was suppressed with the help of Russian troops in 1849. The revolutionary hero then skipped the country and traveled around Europe and America, making a romantic impression on audiences. Austria reasserted control over the damaged territory, and when the Hungarians finally made a peaceful and advantageous settlement with Austria in 1867, resulting in the Dual Monarchy, it was the work, not of a revolutionary but of a Catholic Hungarian patriot, Ferenc Deák.

Various states in Italy had revolts in 1848. They were directed both against Austria, which controlled the north, and toward the goals of liberal republicanism and unification of the peninsula. In Rome, Pope Pius IX had been receptive to liberal ideas, but that was before a revolutionary mob began to swarm around the Vatican. An official standing next to him at his window was shot dead, Pope Pius had to flee Rome for his life, and Napoleon III sent French troops to protect the Papal States. When Pius returned, he was a liberal no longer. (The saying "A conservative is a liberal who has been mugged" seems to apply here.) The movement for Italian unity is overstuffed with colorful characters, and we will follow them to their goal in a subsequent chapter.

In Berlin, Prussia, revolutionaries demanded a liberal constitution in 1848, and there was a movement for German unification. Both the German and Italian unification movements would succeed by the end of the century, with grave consequences for Europe, as we will see. In most other states, even Switzerland, there was some sort of turmoil in 1848;

The Church Under Attack

Metternich's Vienna settlement was not dead yet, but its conservative principles were being steadily eroded.

There was one mid-century revolution that only partially fits the liberal, nationalist, or class-warfare models, and it was the Greek revolt. Greece at the beginning of the century was still under Ottoman Turkish rule, and the Congress of Vienna had not addressed the issue as it worked to preserve the status quo all over Europe. In 1821, a group of Greek patriots in the southern part of the country declared independence from the Turkish Empire, and the Vienna powers were confronted with a dilemma: their goal was to suppress revolution wherever it appeared, but this was a case of Christians trying to throw off the yoke of Europe's historical Muslim enemy. There was a great deal of sympathy for the rebels, both from romantic admirers of classical Greece, such as Lord Byron, and from Catholic France and Orthodox Russia. The Vienna powers refused to suppress the revolt, and with Western aid and encouragement it succeeded in 1832.

Finally, Great Britain did not have a revolution in either 1830 or 1848—it never does, quite—but at times it seemed to be a near thing because of agitation for radical political reforms and the appalling condition of industrial workers. A few wise measures brought some relief, and Great Britain deserves great credit for abolishing slavery, with compensation to the slave owners, all over its empire in 1833. (Imagine if the American colonies had still been part of the empire: our slaves would have been free a whole generation earlier; there would not have been a civil war ...) On the other hand, when the great potato famine struck Ireland in mid-century, England did nothing to alleviate it, partly out of laissez-faire principles, and continued to export food from the island while a million Irish died and another million emigrated. On this bleak note we will pause midway in our survey of the chaotic nineteenth century and take up the remaining threads in a subsequent chapter.

Thought and Culture in the Mid-Nineteenth Century

This period was marked by a bewildering number of political, economic, and social developments that affected culture, as well as the emergence of some major ideologies that are still producing worldwide repercussions. We have already seen a little of the progress of Liberalism, Conservatism, and Romanticism, all of which began before mid-century and continued to develop during the remaining decades. We must now examine the new trends of the period.

The consequences of the Industrial Revolution in every area of life can hardly be exaggerated. The term refers to the shift from agrarian, handicraft production of goods to machine manufacture, division of labor, and urban concentration of factories. It began in the late eighteenth century, but we were busy with Napoleon then and couldn't take a good look at it. Where we are now, around 1840, the revolution is in full swing. It had begun in Britain, where favorable climatic and social conditions (along with the absence of revolutionary turmoil), as well as the Protestant work ethic, led to the development of the cotton industry. Capitalists put up the money, factory owners set up their plants based on Adam Smith's division-of-labor principles, and masses of country people who suddenly found their traditional sources of livelihood drying up flocked to the cities. There they found jobs for barely subsistence wages, at which husbands, wives, and children were all obliged to work long hours at tiresome and often dangerous work. Living conditions were wretched, food and water inadequate or unhealthy, and families often separated. The capitalists who financed the whole thing were, of course, raking in the money.

As for the economists of the day, economic liberalism was their creed. They no longer saw man as a rational animal but as an acquisitive animal driven by the greed and selfishness that made the wonderful technical progress of the machine age possible. "Short-term misery, long-term gain," was their mantra, and I hear it often in the classroom when students kindly point out to me that while the first generations of industrial workers lived short, miserable lives in subhuman conditions, now we have zippers, airplanes, and cell phones. It was worth it.

Dickens did not think it was worth it, and he saw it with his own eyes. (His novels, particularly *Hard Times*, are indispensable reading for a true picture of industrialization in England.) Unlike Dickens, Marx did not care about actual workers—a thoroughgoing idealist, he never seems to have met an actual worker and declined invitations to visit factories, getting all his information from outdated reports—but he saw how their brutalization could produce revolution and eventually his idea of utopia.

Two things might have softened the impact of industrialization and balanced its costs and benefits in a manner befitting human beings. The first thing was the implementation of Catholic principles by the capitalist bosses. This failed because the British capitalists were not Catholic; they were laissez-faire disciples first and often Calvinists second, and for Calvinism the "unsuccessful" workers were merely part of the mass of the unrighteous who were destined for hell anyway. Had they been "saved," they would have been prosperous like their bosses. Secondly, the guilds, which had provided humane working conditions and social benefits for tradesmen of the Middle Ages, had ceased to exist in any meaningful form. Henry VIII and his successors had confiscated whatever funds they had that were in any way related to the guilds' religious functions (Catholic, of course). Since most of the guilds' activities were somehow related to their Catholic principles, they lost so much of their money that their power to assist workers was hopelessly crippled. In France, which became industrialized soon after Britain, the Revolution had already destroyed the guilds, leaving the capitalists a clear field. We will later meet a brilliant bishop, Msgr. Charles-Emile Freppel, who almost single-handedly revitalized the guild system in France and thus greatly improved the condition of both French workers and Catholic employers. But that is in the future. As we survey the polluted landscape, inhuman working conditions, and naked greed of unlovely industrial England, Karl Marx and his English collaborator, Engels (a factory owner himself), are waiting in the wings.

Charles Darwin

Before we get to Marx and Company, we need to meet an Englishman whose work greatly impressed and influenced Marx: Charles Darwin. It should be mentioned here that both Darwinism and Marxism are continuations of the Enlightenment craze for science as well as of that current of Enlightenment thought known as *determinism*. This is the approach to reality that denies free will and assumes some underlying, nonrational mechanism to account for what happens in the world. For Darwin it was evolution, for Marx the class struggle, for Freud (whom we will meet later), subconscious drives within the psyche.

To start with Darwin then: the myth about him is that, through his scientific observations, particularly on his famous voyage to the Galapagos Islands, he acquired data that led him to think that one species could turn into another. This was a purely scientific theory with him, and the evil uses to which it has been put in "social Darwinist" theory would have shocked and depressed him. All this turns out to be wrong. Like Luther with his new religious principles largely worked out long before he posted those theses, Darwin had thought up his evolutionary theories before he ever set foot on the *Beagle* to begin the famous voyage, on which he "discovered" the evidence to support the theory, as ideologues are fond of doing. He himself was also the first Social Darwinist, categorizing the various human races he encountered on his travels as more evolved or less evolved, using criteria such as friendliness to strangers and a work ethic. Implicitly, for Darwin as for his well-heeled followers, the summit of evolution was the Victorian British gentleman.

As for Darwin's thought, it is not free of contradiction and incoherence, especially as he began to perceive how starkly opposed the logical conclusion of his work was to any sort of religion: if all biological change comes about by chance, there is no room for God. If there is no creator guiding the development of life, then life just emerged on its own. Something, in short, came from nothing. A modern analyst of Darwin's works has remarked on how often Darwin insists that "God would not have done it this way," in order to argue his case for blind chance and against God's providence. He seems to have been haunted by God, insisting, for example, that the excessive production by plants of seeds that will never germinate is too wasteful and disorderly to be part of a divine plan. Certainly a tidy, thrifty, Victorian God would "not have done it that way." To illustrate Darwin's theory with an example, we can imagine a herd of quadrupeds in a forest a million or so years ago. They eat the leaves of bushes and low trees. Then there is a drought, the leaves become scarce, and soon all the lower leaves have been eaten and the animals begin to die off. There is a freak among them, however, with an abnormally long neck, and he is able to reach the leaves higher up, so he eats those until the rains come, and he survives. But he is all alone and starts wandering through the woods until he meets another freak like himself: a female freak. They team up, and bingo—you have giraffes, or at least you do in a few hundred thousand years. In such a random and purely accidental way, thought Darwin, all species developed. (Chesterton, however, thought giraffes proved that God has a sense of humor.)

We need not go into the refutation of Darwin's theory, which has been amply accomplished from many angles by many competent writers, with new ones turning up all the time. (See the reading suggestions for a few of them.) We must note here, however, that a scruffy German author wrote to Darwin to say how much he liked his books and to ask if he might dedicate his own book to him. Darwin declined, as most right-thinking people would do, since the German was Karl Marx. What attracted Marx to evolutionary theory? Probably its implicit atheism was not the least of its charms for him, but it also suited quite admirably his theory of class warfare. Darwin had postulated not only the "struggle for survival" and "the survival of the fittest," but their inevitability—an implicit denial both of Providence and of human free will.

Karl Marx

Marx capitalized (if that's not a heretical word to use in connection with him) on the ongoing craze for all things "scientific" by calling his new system "scientific socialism" and studding his explanations of it with supposedly scientific examples, such as the laws of gravity. His other inspiration was the work of Georg Wilhelm Friedrich Hegel, the German idealist philosopher whom Marx so admired that he joined the Young Hegelians at his university when he was a student. Hegel had a theory of Idea as the prime force in history, with one idea (the thesis) being challenged by an opposite idea (the antithesis) and the conflict eventually resulting in a synthesis that would become a new thesis, and so on.

Marx famously said that Hegel had gotten it more or less right but that this dialectic was "standing on its head" and must be put right—by transposing it from the realm of ideas into the realm of matter. His adaptation kept Hegel's schema but substituted human society for abstract ideas, with economics the driving force. Thus in the beginning there was only one class; then the more powerful began to exploit the weaker and make them do their work; the exploited class eventually revolted, defeated their exploiters, and became themselves exploiters. And so on ad infinitum, according to Karl's principles, except that, illogically, he insisted that this "inevitable" process would somehow stop when the proletariat took over the world and set up a classless society (aka utopia). He gave no satisfactory explanation of why the process should ever stop, no matter how nice things would be in the classless utopia.

The whole system is rife with contradictions. Man has no free will, according to Marx the determinist, but somehow he will respond to the Communist Manifesto's call to the workers to throw off their chains. How can he, if he lacks the freedom to decide on an action in the first place? Never mind, it sounds good. Religion, of course, is "the opium of the people," merely one of the tools the exploiting class uses to keep the proletariat in their place; the same goes for culture and the arts, which are only reflections of the exploiters' mentality. (This explains why Soviet Marxism deliberately produced such ghastly sculpture, paintings, and music; they were to reflect the supposedly triumphant proletariat.)

Marx's philosophy is professedly atheistic, but long before he wrote *Das Kapital,* his compendium of Communist ideas, he expressed a very different view in the horrific poems he wrote to Satan — apparently a very real person to Karl Marx — breathing a fanatical hatred of God and mankind. "I want to avenge myself," he wrote, "on Him Who reigns above us." God must have been real to him, at least as the object of his hatred. Other poems reveal a demonic rage and desire to destroy the whole world if he could. Taking the role of God, he screams, "I shall howl gigantic curses at mankind." Once he had thought up Communism, he remarked, "What do I care if three-quarters of the world perish, provided the fourth that is left is Communist?" This creepy versifier was no humanitarian; he had no care for the individual suffering worker and objected when a socialist organization to which he belonged was to be called a "brotherhood." "There are many men," sniffed Marx, "whose brother I do not choose to be." A thoroughly nasty man; he also bullied his wife, had an affair with her servant, and seems to have had unhappy daughters, both of whom later committed suicide.

Ideas Have Consequences

The consequences of the ideas of Darwin and Marx are still with us in many forms. Certainly Marxism is still alive in many political regimes and in universities both here and abroad. As for the ramifications of Darwnism, they are legion. Even in Darwin's lifetime racists seized joyously on this pseudoscientific justification for their views. Victorian explorers and anthropologists saw in primitive peoples survivors of the early stages of human evolution. As one of them wrote, "The savage is morally and mentally an unfit instrument for the spread of civilization.... His place is required for an improved race." (Guess which race? The same one that also felt like that about the Irish.) In Germany, Otto von Bismarck would argue that the death penalty was a means of eliminating the sickly and the effeminate, who would otherwise hold back national development. In the United States in the early twentieth century, a university professor wrote, "The doom that awaits the Negro has been prepared in like measure for all inferior races." It was here too that an African Pygmy, Ota Benga, was displayed like an animal in a zoo; his story is too long to be told here but is worth reading, at least online. We will explore the connection between evolution and Modernism in another chapter.

Chapter 7

The Late Nineteenth Century

In hindsight, many of the political and intellectual developments of the final years of the nineteenth century can be seen
as steps toward the great conflagrations of the early twentieth
century, particularly the Russian Revolution and World War I. I
have not attempted to discuss events all over Europe during this
period — an impossible task — but have tried to focus on those
that had some clear connection with what was to come with
the dawn of the catastrophic twentieth century. It should be
mentioned here that during most of the events reviewed below,
the industrialized West was suffering from a severe depression
that began in 1873 and went on for over twenty years. Economic hardship thus added fuel to increasingly unstable conditions in many countries.

The Adventures of Napoleon III

In the last decades of this century, as in the previous one,
France would again experience both revolution and foreign invasion. Napoleon III was still on the throne in 1870, although
he was not to remain there long. All through his reign he seems
to have hankered after success in war, perhaps out of a desire

to imitate the spectacular successes of his uncle. Napoleon I, however, was a one-of-a-kind military genius, and his nephew fell far short of that.

Part of his problem was the ambivalence of his aims. Like Napoleon I, who had been a Jacobin in his youth, the young Napoleon III had been a member of the revolutionary Carbonari in Italy, much attached to the ideal of Italian nationalism and unification. As emperor, however, we find him sending French troops to protect the pope and Rome from his erstwhile Italian revolutionary colleagues.

He kept trying to have it both ways, going to war with Austria in 1859 in the interests of Italian unification and making a secret deal with the Italian rebel leaders to obtain territory for France if he won. On the other hand, after defeating the Austrians in one battle, he withdrew from the war. He did this so as not to antagonize French Catholics, who were appalled at the revolutionary occupation of the Papal States, although French troops continued to protect Rome itself. The emperor generally tried alternately to placate French liberals, with whom he sympathized, and Catholics, with the result that he was often unpopular with both.

In 1854 he had taken France into the Crimean War when a conflict (which is far too involved to detail here) broke out between Russia and the Ottoman Empire. France, Great Britain, and Sardinia, alarmed at any increase in Russian power, entered the war on the side of the Turks and won. Everyone was surprised that Russia had proved so vulnerable, a conclusion that would later influence the outbreak of World War I. Still, the enterprise had cost roughly two billion dollars and half a million lives—just to prop up a decrepit Turkish empire for a few more years.

The Late Nineteenth Century

Mexican Tragedy

Then Napoleon decided on a Mexican adventure. The corrupt, anti-Catholic government that had resulted from the earlier Mexican revolt against Spain had run up a huge debt to the European powers, causing Great Britain, Spain, and France to invade in 1862 and place the young and idealistic Hapsburg Prince Maximilian and his wife, Charlotte, on the Mexican throne. France's two allies soon withdrew from the enterprise, but French troops managed to capture Mexico City, and the success of the Mexican counterrevolutionaries and the new monarchy seemed within reach. Then came the end of the American Civil War in 1865, and the United States remembered its Monroe Doctrine and began to support the revolutionaries and interfere with French shipments to the Catholic Mexicans and the royal regime.

Despite his promises to the royal couple, whom he had urged to go to Mexico in the first place, Napoleon withdrew French support. Maximilian refused to abandon his Mexican supporters and was captured by the revolutionaries and executed. Before his death Charlotte, who had taken the Spanish name Carlotta, slipped out of the country to seek aid from Europe, but Napoleon refused even to receive her. No other country would help her either, and by the time she finished her trip in Rome, where the pope received her kindly, the strain had caused a permanent mental breakdown. She lived on for many years, apparently never realizing that her husband was dead.

Disaster: The Franco-Prussian War

None of these military enterprises had much of the flavor of the old Grande Armée that had tramped victoriously all over

The Church Under Attack

Europe in the days of the Revolution and Napoleon I. Gone, it seemed, were the days when France had crushed Prussia, that formidable military power. But maybe they were not entirely gone after all, for behold — in 1870 an opportunity arose for a replay of one of those glorious campaigns so popular with the electorate.

The issue was fairly trivial: a relative of Prussian King William I was offered the vacant throne of Spain, and France objected. The French ambassador met with King William at Ems, where His Majesty was vacationing, and the king telegraphed a report of the interview to his prime minister, Bismarck. From the text, it looks as if the ambassador's message was almost insulting, but the prime minister cleverly edited it to read as if the king had snubbed the ambassador, instead of the other way around, and had it published. French public opinion was aroused and, counting on Austrian and Italian help that did not materialize, Napoleon III declared war. He would show those Prussians, the way his uncle did.

Conditions, alas, could not have been more different from those of the late eighteenth century, and there was more than a numerical difference between Napoleons I and III. The Prussia of 1870 had the benefit of the ruthless genius Bismarck, "the Iron Chancellor," who ran the country far more than the king did. For years now he had been militarizing Prussian society intensively, promoting war industries, railroads, and so forth, and working to unite all the German states into one powerful nation, through both diplomacy and war. He had already frustrated some of Napoleon III's plans, and he counted on that doctored telegram to produce the war that would neutralize French rivalry with a united Germany. The fact that France had declared war made her the aggressor in the eyes of even those

Germans who had distrusted the Prussian unification scheme, and they rallied patriotically to Bismarck.

The war ended almost before it really got started. Within the first month, the French were defeated in every battle. The emperor was not well when the time came for him to start for the front, but, apparently urged by his wife, he staggered off in time to be defeated and taken prisoner at the Battle of Sedan. France surrendered, losing the provinces of Alsace and Joan of Arc's Lorraine to the Germans, and gaining nothing but a hefty bill for the costs of the war. The Germans occupied part of France, and, to add insult to injury, Bismarck had his king crowned German emperor in the Hall of Mirrors in the palace of Versailles. French desire for revenge and the recovery of its lost territory would fester until 1914.

Another French Revolution

The unstable situation soon produced yet another revolution in Paris. With the disgrace and departure of Napoleon III and his family, who were soon increasing the deposed-monarch population of England, French politicians formed a parliamentary republican government. It did not satisfy the radicals of Paris, furious over the German victory and the German presence within the country, and they determined to recreate the revolutionary commune of 1792, peculiar calendar and all.

The revolution that erupted in Paris in 1871 was extremely violent; when government forces attempted to enter the capital and restore order, the radicals burned much of the city and massacred their hostages, including the Archbishop of Paris. The citizens, on the verge of starvation, killed and ate the zoo animals. At one point, both the Germans and the de facto French government were besieging the rebels. When it was all over, up to twenty-five thousand people were dead. Political negotiations then began, with the majority of the assembly in favor of monarchy under a grandson of King Charles X. Negotiations broke down, however, and in one key round the proposal for monarchy was defeated by only one vote. The Third French Republic was then firmly established. (The first republic had been set up during the French Revolution and the second followed the Revolution of 1848, before Louis-Napoleon Bonaparte turned it into an empire.) The resulting dreary, corruption-ridden, anti-Catholic regime was to last until 1940.

The Dreyfus Case

Further polarizing and demoralizing French society was a famous espionage case that began in 1894 and dragged on into the following century. Investigation into the passing of secret French documents to the Germans focused, by a process of elimination and handwriting analysis, on Captain Alfred Dreyfus, who happened to be the only Jewish officer on the French general staff. The case is incredibly murky and overcrowded with flamboyant rogues, forged documents, and the suicide of a key figure. Dreyfus was first convicted and sent to Devil's Island prison, then brought back to France for retrial and another, although lesser, conviction and finally pardoned in 1906. He was to fight bravely in the First World War.

The Dreyfus case does not go away. Recent examinations of the evidence have continued to produce a variety of verdicts: Dreyfus was guilty of writing the incriminating documents; he was innocent; he was guilty of writing one of the less important documents, but the others were forged; and so on. Possibly we will never know the truth, but the damage to French society was profound.

Somehow the affair became far more than a spy case, giving birth to anti-Semitic diatribes on the anti-Dreyfus side, and hostility to the French army officers arrayed against him and to their Catholic religion, on the other. Leftists were delighted to have another club with which to bash both the army and the Catholic Church, since most French Catholics were supporters of the military and French officers were largely Catholic. The result was an orchestrated anti-military campaign aimed at discrediting the army, as well as profound discord within French society. This would lead to France's entry into the next war with its people divided and its armed forces demoralized.

Germany

Having dealt effectively with France, Otto von Bismarck now proceeded to shape up internal affairs in the new Germany, and much of what he accomplished in political, economic, military, and diplomatic affairs benefited the country. It also reduced or eliminated the ancient autonomy of the numerous German regions, kingdoms, and principalities, some of them strongly Catholic. The Iron Chancellor wanted a strong, united, and orderly Germany without any tiresome opposition to his policies, and he therefore determined to eliminate as far as possible the political and social influence of the Catholic Church. (This will be discussed in the following chapter.) In the 1880s it was the turn of the Socialists, which led him both to anti-Socialist measures as well as to his own social-justice legislation to reduce the suffering that fed Socialist support. Meanwhile, he made use of secret agents in most states of Europe and negotiated an alliance with Austria and then the Triple Alliance—Germany, Austria, and Italy—in 1882. He worked hard to prevent France—increasingly isolated by the growth of German power—from making an alliance with Russia, a diplomatic revolution that succeeded in spite of him in 1894. These alliances were the beginning of the line-up of powers that would confront each other in World War I.

Bismarck, however, would not be there to see that glorious conflict. A new Kaiser, William II, had come to the throne of Germany in 1888. Twenty-nine years old but possibly somewhat younger in judgment and self-control, he seems to have underrated the treasure he had in his great chancellor and determined to do much of Bismarck's job himself. The two began to clash over matters of policy, in some of which the emperor was inclined to be less ruthless than Bismarck, and at last the great statesman was pressured into resigning in 1890. (He did not go to England.)

Italy

By the end of the nineteenth century, largely as a result of the revolutionary activity that began in 1848, Italy was a united country with a constitutional monarchy. Its revolutionaries had represented varying degrees of radicalism, and some of them appear quite conservative by contrast with the most violent personalities. It is worth mentioning here the phenomenon of Garibaldi, of whom it was said that Italian unity had become his religion. He aroused fanatical devotion in his followers, as illustrated by the recollections of one young man who had fought with him. "He reminded us," gushed this disciple, "of Our Savior.... Everyone said the same. I could not resist him. I went after him. Thousands did likewise. He had only to show himself. We all worshipped him. We could not help it." I mention this as a sample of how the decline of religion is apt to give birth to substitutes that parody some of its features. A secular cause becomes a religion, a revolutionary leader is "worshipped," and his followers actually compare him to Christ. There was more than one such demagogue in the second half of the nineteenth century, but they now appear as mere precursors of the demonic leaders of the twentieth century, possessed of charismatic attraction for great masses of people. Italy would soon become part of the Triple Alliance, with Germany and Austria-Hungary, which would last until World War I.

Austria and Eastern Europe

By the end of the century, Austria had become the Dual Monarchy of Austria-Hungary, with both countries independent entities having a common foreign policy. This had been arranged, after centuries of sporadic Hungarian discontent and rebellion, by the Catholic statesman Ferenc Deák in 1867. The problem of restive minorities within the empire was a headache for both Austria and Hungary, and this was particularly true in South Slav areas such as Bosnia. Bosnia's neighbor, Serbia, was not part of the Austro-Hungarian Empire and in fact had dreams of forming its own Balkan empire. We will see the disaster to which this will lead.

Russia

By the end of the century, Marxist cells were being formed in Russia. They coexisted with other more or less shadowy revolutionary groups of nihilists, anarchists, and a variety of other rebels with a variety of programs. Assassinating the czar was a popular goal with these radicals; it sometimes succeeded, and even when it did not, it caused fear, instability, and increasingly harsh repression by the government. Somewhere in Siberia, at the dawn of the twentieth century, one of the most bizarre and sinister personalities in history was beginning a career that would soon bring him to the center of a world-changing event.

Thought and Culture in the Late Nineteenth Century

The Church was to undergo many trials near the end of the century, as she had at its beginning. As early as 1830, St. Catherine Labouré, even before she received the messages of our Lady concerning the Miraculous Medal, was given to understand that the heart of the founder of her religious order, St. Vincent de Paul, was "deeply grieved by the disasters in store for France." (How the saints, as well as our Lord and our Lady, can be grieved in spite of their possession of eternal bliss, is a mystery. A holy priest once said to me, "Our Lord and our Lady will suffer until the end of the world.") Our Lady referred explicitly to the chastisements awaiting the eldest daughter of the Church: "Great misfortune will come to France: her throne will be overthrown! The whole world will be upset by evils of every kind," she said in 1830, prior to the revolution of that year, which led to the abdication of King Charles X.

About the same time, St. Catherine also had a vision of Christ the King, with his royal insignia falling from him, presaging the fall of the Bourbon king of France. This extraordinary apparition is another indication—like the mission of St. Joan of Arc and the request made of Louis XIV by the Sacred Heart, unfortunately refused—of the predilection of God for the kingdom of France. Later in the month of July 1830, our Lady spoke to St. Catherine of a worse chastisement. In tears, Mary described what was to come: "There will be victims.... There will be victims among the clergy of Paris. Monseigneur the Archbishop.... The cross will be treated with contempt; they will hurl it to the ground. Blood will flow; they will open up again the side of Our Lord. The streets will stream with blood." And Catherine understood that all this would happen in forty years—exactly the date of the revolutionary Commune of 1870 and the martyrdom of the Archbishop of Paris. Our Lady's warnings were not limited to France, however; several times she referred to "the whole world," and she gave the Miraculous Medal to the Church to serve as a remedy and as a stimulus to the devotion of Catholics.

In neighboring Germany, as we have seen, Chancellor Bismarck was ruling with an iron fist during the 1870s, when he began his *Kulturkampf*, or "culture war" against the Catholic Church. This was during the reign of Blessed Pius IX, whose resistance to modern errors had been shown in the *Syllabus*, while papal authority had been upheld by the teaching of Vatican Council I on infallibility. The Church of that time seemed to Bismarck like a threat to his total control of Germany, and persecution was his answer. "We are not going to Canossa," he remarked, alluding to the capitulation of the medieval German emperor Henry IV to Pope Gregory VII. His persecution included expulsion of the Jesuits and suppression of other religious orders, government interference in Catholic education, and anti-Catholic laws affecting the freedom of the Church in Germany. The resistance of Catholic schools, in particular, to the imposition of Bismarck's anti-Catholic ideology was so strong that the tyrant was forced to bring in schismatics such as Old Catholics to keep the system going. At one point over half the bishops were removed from their positions, and some were imprisoned, along with hundreds of priests. The resistance of Catholics did not, however, fade away, as Bismarck had hoped. One prominent bishop who vigorously opposed the control of the state over the Church was Freiherr Wilhelm Emmanuel von Kettler. He was elected as a parliamentary deputy and publicly attacked ideologies at variance with Catholic teaching. His sermons and lectures stimulated the formation of German Catholic social programs designed to cope with the upheavals of industrialization, although he seems to have focused more on trade unions than on the corporatism we will encounter in France. Leo XIII, in fact, used some of Kettler's ideas in his encyclical *Rerum Novarum*. Bishop Kettler died in 1877 while the *Kulturkampf* was still raging, but Bismarck was beginning to realize that his religious policy was a failure. Following the death of Pope Pius IX the following year, he gradually abandoned his domestic "war." By then the more liberal Pope Leo XIII was on the throne and may have seemed less of a threat to the chancellor's iron rule.

The Social Question: France

Meanwhile, poor conditions and unrest among the working classes were fueling Socialist and Communist revolutionary movements. It was imperative that the Church address the plight of the workers from motives of both charity for the poor and concern for order in society. Already Pope Pius IX had issued the first papal statement condemning Communism in 1846, but more was needed. Pope Leo XIII would address the social problem late in the century, but his recommendations represented in some ways a departure from Catholic solutions that had worked admirably in earlier ages and that were being revived in France in the late nineteenth century by an extraordinary bishop, Msgr. Freppel.

There is too much to tell here about this great bishop of Angers, who was repeatedly elected to the French chamber of deputies, where he courageously represented Catholic principles and condemned the errors of the Revolution. He also acted on his principles, publishing brilliant analyses of economic and social questions in the light of the Faith and forming associations of workers and owners of industries to address their problems jointly. (This insistence on a *corporative* approach to the problems of industrialization differs greatly from the concentration on merely forming Catholic labor unions, which often led to further alienation between business owners and their workers. The corporative solution engages the parties involved to solve their problems together.)

Under Freppel's inspiration, which drew extensively on the ideas of the medieval guild system, many initiatives were developed in France to address social issues, ranging from a Catholic workers' placement bureau to a "People's Bank," to trade unions and periodic congresses that were very well attended. When Pope Leo XIII, enamored of "Christian democracy," began to promote ideas and programs at variance with what was already working so well in France, Msgr. Freppel went to Rome to discuss the issues with him, with no result. The new ideas of *Rerum Novarum* and other documents would prevail but would do little to bring together the various units of industrial society, as the guild-inspired movements in France had been doing.

The Church in the late nineteenth century had more than her share of problems to deal with, from revolutionary ideologies to social problems to active persecution by hostile governments. As if these were not enough, the most formidable development of all began to loom on the horizon.

Modernism

We shall see in a later chapter the reaction of the Church to this "compendium of all heresies" and the masterly analysis of it by Pope St. Pius X, but the seeds of this slippery ideology were already sprouting as the nineteenth century neared its close. Modernism appeared first in nineteenth-century Protestant thought and is often known as "liberal Christianity." One of its manifestations was a tendency to "demythologize" Scripture, largely by explaining away the miracles, as Thomas Jefferson had done in the previous century, and focusing on religious experiences instead of dogma.

Modernism has been called the application of Darwinism to religion, and the description seems apt. For evolutionists, nature is viewed as in a state of flux, with things always evolving into other things (never mind that we somehow don't see this happening). Similarly, Modernists see dogma in a state of flux as human consciousness evolves and the religious "community" comes to see spiritual truths in new ways. How often have we heard, in the aftermath of the Second Vatican Council that lifted the rocks and allowed hibernating Modernism to seep forth once again, "Well, we used to think this, but *now* we think that."

Nineteenth-century Modernism, having colonized Protestant thought, would begin to infiltrate Catholic minds on the other side of the year 1900. We will take up that distressing development shortly.

Saints and More Saints

Despite the catastrophic events and ominous developments of the nineteenth century, or probably because of them, God raised up more saints than could possibly be mentioned here. I am limiting this short section to two saints known, like St. Catherine Labouré, for their prophecies of future disasters for the Church and the world. St. John Bosco is very well known, but his many visions—some of them prophetic, like those of St. Catherine—are less so. Perhaps the best known of his "dreams" is the one he had in 1862 that seems to be a figurative representation of a great crisis in the Church, seen as a naval battle. A pope is on the flagship, where he first falls wounded, then recovers, and finally is struck again and killed. A new pope is elected so quickly that "the news of the death of the Pope coincides with the news of the election of the successor." The battle is finally won and the enemy routed, as the papal ship and its allies come to anchor between two great pillars, one bearing the Host and the other a statue of our Lady.

Don Bosco did not comment on the pope who had died, but he did explain that the enemy ships represented persecutions. "The most serious trials for the Church are near at hand. That which has been so far is almost nothing in the face of that which must befall.... Only two means are left ... devotion to Mary Most Holy and Frequent Communion, making use of every means and doing our best to practice them and having them practiced by everyone." He did not explain further, although it was later said that on one pillar he had seen the date 1571, the year of the naval victory of Lepanto against the Ottoman Turks. Some details of the vision do not appear to have yet come to pass, although certainly the atrocities of the Paris Commune and other worse persecutions of the Church throughout the world have occurred since 1862.

St. Anthony Mary Claret of Spain was born in 1807 and died in 1870. A great preacher, both in Europe and in Cuba (where several attempts were made to murder him), writer, and founder of the Claretians, St. Anthony was one of the great Marian saints, consecrated to the Immaculate Heart of Mary. In this he seems to anticipate our Lady's requests at Fatima, and her plea for the establishment of the devotion to her Immaculate Heart alongside that of the Sacred Heart of Jesus. Among the many supernatural messages he received from our Lord and prophecies of events that later occurred is one in which Christ refers to "the immense chastisements soon to come to pass." St. Anthony was then given to understand a passage from the book of Revelation—also cited by Sister Lucia of Fatima—that mentions three angels who will sound trumpets. St. Anthony saw these as "the three great judgments of God which are going to fall upon the world." They are "1) Protestantism and Communism; 2) the four arch demons who will, in a truly frightful manner, incite all to the love of pleasure, money, reason and independence of will; 3) the great wars with their horrible consequences."

We cannot say we have not been warned by divine messages, many times over, of the chastisements coming because of our sins. We will witness some of them in the twentieth century.

Chapter 8

The Century of Total War: Part One

The turn of the century, including the 1890s on one side and the early 1900s on the other, was in some respects a giddy and optimistic period. Science and technology fueled dreams of ever-increasing prosperity; long-distance travel became easier and more common, and new popular music and other forms of entertainment became more accessible to the masses. People looked forward to a happy and peaceful age of progress. But what of the horrible vision of Satan and the diabolical onslaught of about a hundred years in duration revealed to Pope Leo XIII in 1884? And how could Pope St. Pius X wonder, in 1903, whether "the Son of Perdition spoken of by the Apostle might already be living on this earth?"

As things turned out, of course, optimism about the new age was wildly misplaced, and the twentieth century produced one nightmare after another of unprecedented horror and suffering. Even before the outbreak of the First World War, several heads of state in both Europe and America had been assassinated by anarchists, and underground revolutionary movements were gaining ground in several countries. Relations between the militantly secular French state and the Church worsened; religious orders were persecuted and their schools closed, while competent Catholic army officers were replaced with men chosen by anticlerical politicians. Various crises began to absorb the attention of some of the states of Europe, but few saw them as portents of a future cataclysm. Japan launched a surprise attack on Russia in 1904 and had defeated her by 1905. That the great empire of the czars could be defeated that fast by such a small opponent was a shock to the Russians as well as everybody else and gave the diplomats of Europe much food for thought. The disruptions produced by the war caused food shortages and agrarian turmoil within Russia in the aftermath of the war, culminating in an outbreak of revolution in 1905.

The Balkan powder keg, true to form, sputtered ominously in the early twentieth century, as the Balkan Wars finally expelled the Ottoman Turks from Europe. Serbia had plans for an empire of its own on the ruins of the Turkish one, and the Turks themselves lurched from insurrection to revolution as the remnants of their empire from Libya to Crete to the Balkan Peninsula disappeared.

Austria-Hungary faced the problem of increasingly militant minorities within its borders, all demanding some form of autonomy, regardless of their capacity for independent existence. Germany after Bismarck was more militant (and militarized) than ever, building a fleet to rival that of Great Britain and making an alliance with Italy and Austria-Hungary—and later with Turkey—to counter the diplomatic "understanding" (entente) among Great Britain, France, and Russia. Most of the states mentioned so far, as well as others such as Belgium and Holland, also had colonial enterprises in which each was the rival of all the others. *Peaceful* was not the best word for that charming world of the waltz, the operetta, and the horseless carriage.

The Century of Total War: Part One

The Great War

This cataclysm, which would come to be called the First World War when the second one occurred, seems to have been to the West a shock for which no one was prepared. Its origin recalled the beginning of the last great European War, the Thirty Years' War, which had begun four hundred years earlier, in 1618. The earlier conflict had begun when Bohemia, in Eastern Europe, had revolted against Hapsburg rule. The Great War began when a member of a Serbian revolutionary group, the Black Hand, assassinated a Hapsburg grand duke in Austrian-controlled Bosnia. In both cases, the Austrians tried to deal with what appeared to be a purely regional issue, only to find that other countries began to join the fray as soon as it got going.

We cannot get into the details of World War I here, but they are readily accessible in any textbook. Austria wanted Serbia to hand over or punish the group of assassins and claimed the right to enter Serbia and oversee the effort. Serbia, however, hoping to form its own Balkan empire and eliminate the Austrian presence there, began to mobilize, counting on its ally Russia for support. When the Serbs rejected the Austrian ultimatum, Austrian ships shelled Belgrade, pointing out that they were not invading Serbian territory; certainly they did not want the situation to escalate and bring Russia into the affair, but they also knew they were backed up by their ally, Germany. Russia had begun to mobilize partially, since Czar Nicholas II hoped that that would deter further Austrian aggression. His general staff persuaded him to order complete mobilization, to which Austria responded by also mobilizing fully. France, England, and other states scrambled to form their own policies. Austria's ally, Germany, then ordered Russia to stop mobilization within twelve hours (which was impossible, even had Russia been willing). When this demand was not met, Germany declared war on August 1 and began to implement a battle plan previously worked out that involved attacking France through Belgium and Luxembourg.

Incredibly, the Western powers were unprepared for this development, despite the many diplomatic and military danger signals that had been issuing from Germany. There was great enthusiasm for war, nevertheless, in the major capital cities such as Paris and London. The French in particular were eager to revenge their defeat in the Franco-Prussian War and recover Alsace-Lorraine. The Great War, however, would be different from anything seen before in Europe. There are accounts of young French cavalry officers, laughing and waving their swords, and charging German lines, only to meet instant death: no one had told them about the new machine guns. Poison gas was another new weapon the efficient Germans utilized, and their tanks were mechanized monsters no other country could match. Long-term trench warfare was a major feature of the war, which everyone had originally thought would be over in a few weeks. The casualty figures from even one period of the four-year war are staggering: from March to December 1916, the stalemate between the Germans and French near Verdun caused an estimated four hundred thousand deaths, while nearly twice that number of men were gassed or wounded. Between July and December of that same year, at the Battle of the Somme, Britain, France, and Germany suffered over one million casualties, yet the battle line moved only seven miles—that was two and a half deaths per inch.

Nations switched sides or withdrew during the four long years of war. Italy left the Triple Alliance, in which it had been a partner with Austria-Hungary and Germany, and went over to the Allies in 1915. Russia, following the revolution that we will shortly examine, withdrew from the war in 1917, while the United States entered it in early 1918. From the beginning, a negotiated peace should have been possible. It would have left the German military discredited but the imperial government intact, which could well have prevented the later rise of Hitler. Germany, however, wanted a decisive defeat of Great Britain and France and was not open to negotiation; on their side, the Allies had promised land to Italy if she would desert her allies in 1915 and needed more time to fulfill that promise. They also wanted a decisive victory over Germany and were not inclined to compromise. Pope Benedict XV certainly urged peace, but he was seen as pro-German, and the French resented his refusal to admit the greater guilt of Germany in invading small, defenseless neighbors such as Belgium and Luxembourg. He was given to urging vague, idealistic schemes of general disarmament, which were totally unrealistic and unhelpful in the circumstances.

A Tragic Emperor

The only head of state who was actively trying to promote peace on a practical level was the new, young emperor of Austria-Hungary. Franz Joseph had died at last in 1916, after a very long reign: he had first come to the throne during the revolutions of 1848. His family seemed to be stalked by violence. In 1853, he was the victim of an assassination attempt by a revolutionary who tried to stab him, but he was saved by an unlikely team of an Irish count and a passing Austrian butcher. (Both were rewarded, with the butcher becoming a nobleman.) One by one he had seen his heirs die violent deaths. His only son, Rudolf, was either murdered or committed suicide at Mayerling in 1889; one of his brothers, Maximilian, had been executed in Mexico some decades earlier, and another died of water poisoning while on pilgrimage to the Holy Land. His beloved wife, Elizabeth, was stabbed to death by an anarchist in 1898, while the death of his nephew, Archduke Franz Ferdinand, had touched off the Great War. Now at last the old emperor himself was gone, leaving as heir his grandnephew Karl (who was beatified in 2004). Karl was willing to negotiate with the Allies and even surrender some Austrian territory in the cause of peace, but he met with no cooperation from the great powers. His messages to the French government went unanswered. President Wilson, an idealist with an antipathy to monarchy, would not even listen to his proposals—apparently on the grounds that he had not been elected. And so the war continued its murderous course until the armistice in 1918. We will consider the peace settlements in the next chapter.

The Communist Revolution in Russia

There is more than one resemblance between the French Revolution of 1789 and the Russian Revolution of 1918, and some of the participants seemed very conscious of the fact. Lenin asked, as the revolution began to succeed, "Where are we going to get our Fouquier-Tinville?" That sinister figure was public prosecutor during the Terror, legendary for his cruel dedication to the revolutionary cause.

The myth about the Russian Revolution holds that the Russian people were so poor and miserable that they finally threw off their chains, overthrew their oppressive government, and liberated themselves. Nothing is further from the truth. In the first place, as we have seen before, it is never "the people" who make revolutions; in the second place, Russia in the decade

The Century of Total War: Part One

before the Great War was experiencing, in spite of the troubles caused by the Russo-Japanese War of 1905, an unprecedented prosperity. This was due largely to a brilliant and practical czarist official named Pyotr Stolypin. He managed to change the age-old, stagnant, and highly inefficient peasant system wherein farmers' lands were not their own but were those of the hidebound village communes. Stolypin's scheme of privatization of peasant holdings worked so well that peasants in 1913 were soon outproducing the larger landowners and pushing them out of the market. Not only did domestic consumption rise, but exports also increased—by a whopping 61 percent over the early years of the century. Peasant savings greatly increased too, and foreign investors flocked to Russia. Tragically, before Stolypin was finished with his great plans for the Russian economy, he was shot by a revolutionary assassin while at the opera in 1911. He made the Sign of the Cross, saluted the czar, who was in the royal box, and died saying, "I am happy to die for the czar."

Stolypin was practically irreplaceable, and as revolutionary agitation increased and the country lurched into World War I, a new and demonic personality gained the confidence of the royal family and perhaps did more than Lenin or Trotsky to destroy the Russia of the czars. He seemed to have paranormal powers and had in fact prophesied Stolypin's death; his name was Rasputin. The czar was a mild man, unwilling to oppose his strong-willed wife in anything, so when the supposed holy man Rasputin proved able to arrest the bleeding of their hemophiliac son, Czarina Alexandra was willing to do anything he said—and to see that her husband did so also. Even as the czar was with the troops at the front and the war was going badly for Russia, competent governmental ministers were being replaced by worthless cronies of Rasputin. He was finally killed—by a group of noblemen who saw no other way to save Russia — in the course of a long and hideous night during which he was thought to have died several times, only to pop back up so that all the nasty, weary work had to be done over again.

The death of one of the strangest characters in history did not, of course, save Russia. It was far too late for that, and the abdication of the czar and the establishment of a provisional leftist government did not bring stability either. Lenin's Communists took power in October (November in our calendar) of 1917. One of Lenin's first moves was to take Russia out of the war, at the price of a large amount of territory ceded to the Central Powers. The czar and his family were first imprisoned in March 1917, while the revolutionaries debated on whether and when to kill them. It was over a year later, in July 1918, that Lenin finally gave the order for the execution of the whole family. The royal family, their children, and their servants were gruesomely slain; several died slowly of stab wounds or multiple gun shots. The Soviet Union had begun.

Thought and Culture in the Century of Total War

The greatest evil to afflict the Church in the early twentieth century was Modernism, which we encountered briefly when it began to emerge in the late nineteenth century. The greatest consolation of the Church in the twentieth century was, or should have been and should still be, Fatima. We will examine the early history of both these phenomena and will meet them again in later twentieth-century history.

Modernism

We noticed the first rumblings of Modernist thought in those nineteenth-century Protestants who began applying Darwinism to religion. If religion evolved like everything else, it was no longer necessary to believe in fixed doctrines. Modernism was "the compendium of all heresies," as St. Pius X was to call it.

The French priest Father Alfred Loisy, one of its leading exponents, wrote some of the first books by a Catholic (at least he was one for a while) that would spread Modernism in Catholic seminaries, schools, and minds. The influence of the liberal Protestant Modernist Adolf von Harnack on Fr. Loisy is just one example of the seeping of the original Protestant version of this insidious heresy into the Catholic Church. The budding French Modernist argued that Harnack had been partially right in his theory that our Lord had not intended to form an organized church—at least not the way it was organized, so inconveniently for Father Loisy, in his own day. He thought that Christ could not know how the Church would change after he had left the earth; he also held that Christ did not know he was consubstantial with the Father, an idea that came from the much later Council of Nicaea. (The idea that our Lord did not know who he was or what the future was to be, or really much of anything, is still found among "liberal" Catholics.) Loisy also wrote, in 1904, that he considered "the virgin birth and the resurrection to be purely moral symbols."

For Modernists, everything we thought we believed was actually only provisional, since dogma "evolves" constantly. Each new generation must discover and create its own theological notions, because solemnly defined doctrines are silly and out of date. It is not difficult to see how such thinking could destroy the faith in countless souls. Loisy's influence spread, not only in France but in England, where his best-known followers were Baron Friedrich von Hügel and the Jesuit Father George Tyrrell.

The Church Under Attack

Accession of St. Pius X

Pope St. Pius X succeeded Leo XIII in 1903. He had no illusions about the growing crisis in the Church and the world, and in his first encyclical, *E supremi apostolatus* (On the Restoration of All Things in Christ), he referred to his "terror" at the appalling condition of mankind due to its apostasy from God. He characterized it as "this monstrous and detestable iniquity proper to the times we are living in, and through which man substitutes himself for God." He wondered, too, "whether such a perversion of minds is not the sign announcing, and the beginning of, the last times, and that the Son of Perdition spoken of by the Apostle [II Thess. 2:3] might already be living on this earth."

Not one to tolerate the poisoning of the Catholic well by heretics, he began to place Modernist writings on that very useful — but now abolished — index of books forbidden to Catholics. This did not destroy Modernism, although it limited the exposure of the ordinary faithful to it; possibly its adherents — who represented more of an intellectual clique than a popular movement — drew comfort from seeing themselves as noble victims of obscurantism. In any case, they did not disappear or repent. Like heretics in the past, they wanted to eliminate many popular devotions dear to the unenlightened masses, and to "democratize" Church government. They wanted a poorer and simpler clergy, and Loisy himself seems to have been for changing the requirement of clerical celibacy. In connection with this, Paul Hallett has written that, "the Modernist principle of Vital Immanence, which makes conscience autonomous, is tailor-made for a softening in sexual teaching." (Vital Immanence is the idea that the divine principle is located within, not outside, man, and is the source of his religious and moral beliefs.)

The Century of Total War: Part One

Sources of Modernist Theories

Most of these ideas can be found in heretical movements from the Middle Ages through the Reformation, when they produced organized new sects. What was new — and formidable — about Modernism, it seems to me, was precisely its espousal of the new theory of evolution in regard to doctrine. The Modernist idea is that Church doctrine is constantly evolving according to the circumstances of each subsequent Christian community, and this process is inevitable. As with the Marxist class struggle, change is relentlessly ongoing and cannot be halted. Marx's problem was that he wanted it to stop once it had achieved a classless utopia, but the Modernists do not seem to have foreseen any stopping point. The inevitability of the great evolution of dogma and practice increased the exalted zeal, fanaticism, and dedication of the religious revolutionaries. They were part of a *Zeitgeist* greater than themselves, of which they were both the instruments and the missionaries.

The Anti-Modernist Offensive of St. Pius X

The campaign of Pope Pius, which had been gathering steam since the beginning of his reign, reached its high point in 1907. In July of that year, the Holy Office issued the decree *Lamentabili*, sometimes referred to as "the new *Syllabus*," condemning sixty-five Modernist propositions. The same year saw a number of other measures against various Modernist publications, and the excommunication of their authors; Loisy himself would be excommunicated the following year. In September 1907, the landmark encyclical *Pascendi* was published. This brilliant and thorough analysis of the Modernist heresy is well worth studying; the condemnation of the theories discussed is quite clear, and it was emphasized and reinforced in subsequent papal documents. Both *Lamentabili* and *Pascendi* appear to be infallible exercises of the Magisterium. The anti-Modernist oath was decreed in *Pascendi*, and all priests, bishops, and teachers were required to take it until it was abolished by Pope Paul VI—either because he thought it was no longer needed or because we had all become Modernists despite it. As we know, at that point the Modernists pushed up the rocks under which they had been lying dormant since the early part of the century, and slithered forth. Their writings have proliferated since Vatican II, and I have had the penance of reading many of them recently as we were setting up our parish library and weeding out the junk. It is an encouraging sign, however, that the junk is beginning to seem dated while traditional teaching is still persuasive. Certainly the Modernists would never have dreamed that their sacred evolution might end in a return to Tradition; the very thought would have made them sick. It would be like the French revolutionaries watching "the people" they had idolized vote for a king.

Fatima

What follows concerning this most important event, the greatest apparition of our Lady in modern times and, according to Sister Lucia, the last, is a very brief summary, because the whole story of these visits of our Lady, her messages, and the lives of the three children who saw her would require volumes. The best account, in fact, is the multivolume work *The Whole Truth about Fatima*, by Brother Michel de la Sainte Trinité and Brother François des Anges. Here we are going to look at some key themes of the messages and, in particular, their intimate connection with historical events—unprecedented in the history of Marian apparitions. According to some theologians, in fact, the phenomena of Fatima do not strictly belong to the category of "private revelation" because of the nature of the messages and the spectacular and public miracle by which they were validated.

Our Lady's Response to the War and the Revolution

As events in twentieth-century Europe, and indeed the world, spiraled out of control over the edge of an abyss of suffering, the Blessed Virgin Mary entered the fray in the most spectacular series of heavenly visitations in history. As Sister Lucia would tell Father Augustine Fuentes in a conversation in 1957: "In the plans of Divine Providence, God always, before he is about to chastise the world, exhausts all the other remedies. Now, when he sees that the world has not heeded any of them, then, as we say in our imperfect manner of speaking, he offers us with a certain trepidation, the last means of salvation, his most holy Mother."

The terrible chastisements we have briefly considered were thus accompanied by extraordinary visits of our Lady to a small Portuguese town with a message for the world and for the popes. In 1916, prior to the appearance of our Lady herself, an angel calling himself the Angel of Peace and the Angel of Portugal—identified with St. Michael—came several times to three young Portuguese shepherd children: Lucia, Jacinta, and Francisco. He taught the children prayers of reparation and urged them to make sacrifices for the conversion of sinners, with particular emphasis on the "outrages, sacrileges, and indifferences" by which our Lord is offended. He referred to the Holy Eucharist as "horribly outraged by ungrateful men." Then on May 13, 1917, Mary herself appeared to the children for the first time, promising to return on the thirteenth day of the next five months.

The Messages and the Miracle

The child-seers of Fatima knew that a war had begun in 1914, although they were unaware of developments in Russia and probably did not even know where and what it was. Their lives now centered on their monthly rendezvous with the Blessed Mother. In the first apparition, on May 13, 1917, she taught them a prayer and asked them to say the Rosary and sacrifice for sinners and to pray for the end of the war. In June, during her second visit, she announced that God wanted to establish on earth the devotion to the Immaculate Heart of Mary. The third apparition, in July, included the famous vision of hell and the mysterious "Third Secret" that the children were not to reveal until much later. It also included a promise that the war was going to end, but that if men did not stop offending God,

another and worse war will break out in the reign of Pius XI. When you see the night illumined by an unknown light, know that it is the great sign that God gives you that He is going to punish the world for its crimes by means of war, hunger, persecution of the Church and of the Holy Father. To forestall this, I shall come to ask the consecration of Russia to my Immaculate Heart and the Communion of Reparation on the first Saturdays. If they heed my request, Russia will be converted and there will be peace. If not, she shall spread her errors throughout the world, promoting wars and persecutions of the Church; the good will be martyred and the Holy Father will have much to suffer, various nations will be annihilated; in the end, my Immaculate Heart shall triumph. The Holy Father will consecrate Russia to me, which will be converted, and some time of peace will be given to the world.

Our Lady further promised that in October she would tell the children her name and what she wanted and would perform a miracle that all would see. In the following two months, our Lady repeated some of her earlier instructions, continued to urge prayer and penance, and mentioned again what she would do on October 13. When that day came, she referred to herself specifically as the Lady of the Rosary and promised that the war would end and the soldiers would soon be home. She also spoke again of how much our Lord was offended by sin and the need for people to reform their lives and recite the Rosary daily.

On October 13, 1917, the children alone saw our Lady. In addition, however, they saw a marvelous series of tableaux in which St. Joseph also appeared. Suddenly, in full view of between fifty thousand and seventy thousand witnesses, who had come from Portugal as well as all of Europe, the famous Miracle of the Sun took place. The sun seemed to spin in the sky, emitting colored rays, and then plunged toward the earth, terrifying the spectators, before returning to its normal place and state. We have the report of an agnostic reporter for a Socialist newspaper who had gone prepared to write an account of a fraud and had to admit that he had seen a miracle. With commendable honesty, he described it in detail in his article. The testimony of this skeptical witness, added to the fact that people miles away from the site also witnessed it, rules out mass hallucination. Our Lady had provided spectacular proof of the genuineness of her message.

The Church Under Attack

Aftermath

The people of Fatima did take our Lady's message to heart, at least for a time, and she kept her promise. Portugal had been neutral at the outbreak of the Great War, but in 1916 she had complied with a British request to seize German ships in Portuguese ports and sell them to Great Britain. This brought a declaration of war against Portugal from Germany and Austria-Hungary, so the small country was now obliged to send its soldiers to fight the Germans on two fronts: in its East African colonies and in France. The first Portuguese casualty in France occurred in April 1917, the month before the Blessed Virgin's first visit to the children. The war ended the following year.

As for the rest of Christendom and our Lady's further requests, they will be discussed in a later chapter.

Chapter 9

The Century of Total War: Part Two

In the course of the twentieth century, our Lady's requests would not be fulfilled and all her prophecies would come true, as we will see. The Communist Empire took hold in Russia with only a feeble attempt at intervention by the Allies as World War I ended in 1918. In that same year, the greatest influenza pandemic in history struck the world. Millions of people worldwide perished of the disease, sometimes within twenty-four hours. An unknown number also died of secondary infections or complications of the flu. Most American war casualties were due to the influenza, not combat.

Peace Breeds War

The 1919 peace settlement that followed the defeat of the Central Powers in the previous year was a recipe for further conflict. Unlike the provisions of the Congress of Vienna in 1815, which dealt leniently with defeated France (the country that gave us the wars of the French Revolution and Napoleon, which together cost Europe millions of lives and massive destruction), the World War I treaties were unnecessarily vindictive and harsh. Much of the blame goes to the Calvinist and liberal ideologue Woodrow Wilson, who hated what he called "autocracy." Having made, as he thought, "a world safe for democracy," Wilson wanted to make sure both that it *was* democratic and that there was an international structure to guarantee the safety of the new world order. The League of Nations was the embodiment of Wilson's dream. In a little more than a decade, it would be an irrelevant failure, while poor Wilson undermined his own health trying to persuade his isolationist countrymen to support it, ultimately dying without succeeding.

Two of the great monarchies of Europe, the Hohenzollerns in Germany and the Hapsburgs in Austria-Hungary, traditional elements of stability within their territories, were removed from power. Nobody wanted the German Kaiser William II to stick around, of course. He retired to Holland, where he continued to annoy his family, in one instance by unexpectedly marrying a servant girl. There were, however, other members of his family who could have ruled—and stabilized—a country that had never known another form of government. (The wise Congress of Vienna had allowed the Bourbons to continue to rule France after its defeat.)

A catastrophic rearrangement of the map of Europe came out of the peace settlement, based partly on a desire to punish the losing side as no enemy, except perhaps Carthage in Roman times, had ever been punished, and partly on Wilson's fanatical dedication to the "self-determination of peoples" based on ethnicity or—if that proved too murky—on a common language. Hungary, Austria's partner in the Austro-Hungarian Empire, had had self-government within the empire but not an independent foreign policy. Never mind; it would be punished for Austrian policies by the loss of two-thirds of its ancient territory—exorbitant by any standards of retribution.

The Century of Total War: Part Two

Of course, Wilson's dedication to tribalism operated here, because the areas that were lopped off Hungary were organized into states according to ethnic or linguistic criteria. Thus, Rumania was given the large Hungarian area of Transylvania, on the pretext that it was full of Rumanians. Areas where Slovaks lived, including the medieval Hungarian capital of Pozsony, were detached from Hungary, although Wilson did not leave it at that. Because Slovaks and Czechs both spoke a Slavic language, despite their many other differences, including religion, Wilson glued them together in a new creation: Czechoslovakia. For the same reason he formed Yugoslavia of several very different ethnic and religious groups. All over Eastern Europe small, unstable states were set up and told to form democracies, whether they wanted to or not. Wilson considered putting the German-speaking, ethnically related states of Germany and Austria together but seems to have been deterred by the idea that that would somehow create a large Catholic power in the middle of Europe influenced by the papacy. Truncated Austria had to become a republic. Self-determination somehow did not apply to Ukraine, which wanted freedom from Soviet control; the Ukrainians were told just to trust the new League of Nations. The league, however, had just given Upper Silesia and its German population to Poland, so what its operating principles actually were remained unclear.

It should have been obvious that small, new states with unfamiliar governmental systems would be vulnerable to conquest by the next great power, and so it happened: they would fall first to a resurgent Germany and then to the Soviet Union. Bitter resentment at the injustice of the territorial and governmental conditions imposed would produce in some cases revolutions and in others a willingness to join whatever power would promise a new deal. In the European areas where the war had been fought (which ironically did not include Germany, which saw no major fighting on its soil) massive destruction had occurred, and all countries involved in the war also suffered unprecedented numbers of casualties: half the young men of France—two million of them—perished or were maimed. Hard on the heels of the closing battles of the war came the influenza epidemic of 1918, unwittingly brought by American troops from Kansas, where it had begun as a bird flu that mutated into a swine flu, and mutated again into its deadliest form in Europe. Worldwide it affected close to a billion people, of whom twenty to forty million died; 85 percent of American war dead (forty-three thousand) died of influenza.

The Suffering of Germany

Inflation was rampant in most European countries following the war. Germany was hardest hit, since the crushing amount of reparations it was assessed overtaxed an economy unable to deal with the costs of defeat. In 1923, an obscure failure of a painter attempted to take power by ranting and raving in a Bavarian beer hall. He was imprisoned and spent his jail time writing a book called *Mein Kampf*, laying out a detailed program that he would later follow to the letter when he came to power. Too bad that apparently no government figures, either inside or outside Germany, bothered to read it. By the mid-1920s, recovery was underway in Germany, partially stimulated by American investment and economic aid, and Germany was admitted to the League of Nations in 1926. Then came the Great Depression of 1929, and American investment ceased. All countries, except for the Soviet Union, suffered from this capitalist collapse, with massive unemployment and general economic disarray everywhere. In Germany, the unstable situation brought that scribbling ex-jailbird first into the government and then to the presidency—with 88 percent of the vote. His name, of course, was Adolf Hitler.

Hitler proceeded to turn the German economy around within weeks; he built the great highway system, called for the development of a "people's car" (the Volkswagen), and built up the military within the strict limits of the Versailles Treaty. By a secret agreement with the Soviet Union he also developed tanks, the air force that the Allies had forbidden, and poison-gas research in clandestine installations on Russian soil. By a series of steps, including organizing Nazi groups within Austria and sending his army across the German-Austrian border just before a plebiscite was to be held on Austrian independence, he took over the country, quoting Wilson's principle that ethnically and linguistically identical people should be in the same state. He also scooped up the German area of Czechoslovakia (the Sudetenland), and then the whole country. When he attacked Poland in 1939, with his ally Stalin attacking from the east so that each of them would get half, the Allies—primarily Great Britain and France at this point—belatedly decided to stop him; World War I had not been the "war to end all wars" after all.

The Second Great War

Nothing much happened in the first year of the war, and people began to refer to a "phony war." France was totally unprepared for war, despite the repeated pleas of Marshal Pétain, hero of World War I, for military modernization. A pacifist, Socialist-dominated government was in power during the thirties, and the indecisive and frightened men in power when Hitler unleashed his 1940 "lightning war" in all directions wanted to unload responsibility for the ensuing debacle. Incredibly, they had counted on a series of fortifications on the eastern border known as the Maginot Line to protect France from invasion; the Germans simply went around it. After a solemn—and laughable, considering their atheist and Masonic sentiments—pilgrimage to Notre Dame, to show they were trying everything, the government members voted to turn over power to Marshal Pétain, then in his late seventies. One-third of France was in the process of being occupied by the enemy, including Paris. Hundreds of thousands of French soldiers would end up in German camps. This civilian and captured military population would constitute many hostages whose lives depended on what the marshal would do.

Pétain realized that France could not possibly continue fighting; a young, hotheaded, and insubordinate soldier named Charles de Gaulle argued that with the French army in Africa continued resistance was possible. Pétain, with vastly more military experience, judged that that part of the army needed to be built up considerably before any confrontation with the Germans was possible, and to gain time he signed an armistice with Hitler. The unoccupied southern part of France would remain so; it included the Mediterranean coast, which Hitler wanted and would not get—some historians thus consider the armistice a very costly blunder for him. The new French government was headquartered at Vichy, in the south, and had the support of almost the entire French population. Marshal Pétain was of peasant origin, a Catholic, and determined to give the French people an orderly conservative government. He reduced the power of the large capitalists and favored a corporatist organization of the economy; he appointed as minister of agriculture the first peasant to hold that position; he supported the Catholic Church and her institutions. All this was a breath of fresh air for a country long subjected to anti-Catholic and frequently oppressive rule. There was a price, of course: neutrality in the war and cooperation with Germany. French factories had to produce quotas for the Germans, although they did so as slowly as they could, and some demands were refused. It was a fine line. At one point, when someone asked the marshal about ignoring a German demand, he reminded the questioner that the Germans were capable of executing the entire population of the province of Alsace. Hitler never got the Mediterranean coast or the French fleet; when the Germans finally overran the whole country later in the war, the Pétain government gave orders that the fleet should be scuttled rather than fall into German hands. Pétain had also arranged for the French army in Africa, which he continued to build up secretly, to join the Allies during the final offensives of the war.

The American ambassador to Vichy was much impressed with the marshal and admired him greatly. Pétain was also in oral communication with Churchill; their messages were transmitted through secret agents who memorized and delivered them, leaving nothing in writing. In England, however, was the French defector de Gaulle, now broadcasting to the world that he represented the "free French" and calling for resistance to the Germans in France. The myth of the Resistance would take too long to demolish here. Suffice it to say that while this underground movement devoted to sabotaging German operations in France certainly included men and women of goodwill, it also included plenty of men with a political agenda for the postwar period. During the war, they caused much havoc to their French countrymen because of the reprisals their actions elicited: the Germans retaliated on innocent civilians, in one case machine-gunning an entire village, for damage done by the Resistance. We will follow the fortunes of the Resistance and the marshal in the postwar period later.

Meanwhile, most of Europe was occupied by the Germans; they were welcomed in parts of Eastern Europe because Hitler had promised the restoration of territory stolen from them after World War I. So far Hitler was behaving like Napoleon; he behaved even more like him when he invaded his former ally the Soviet Union, with predictably disastrous results. At the end of 1941, the Japanese attack on Pearl Harbor had brought the United States into the war, and 1942 would see the turning of the tide against Hitler.

The three great turning points of the war in that year were the Soviet defeat of the Germans at Stalingrad, the British victory over German troops at El Alamein in Egypt, and the American destruction of the Japanese fleet at Midway. The roll-back of the German armies continued until Berlin was taken in 1945; in a fateful decision, the American troops held back their offensive on the city so that Soviet troops could occupy it. The Russians were already all over Eastern Europe, with the goal of setting up Soviet regimes everywhere. Tragically, the year that saw victory against Germany also saw the start of that tense state of hostility between the Soviet Union and the West known as the Cold War, which will be discussed in the next chapter.

War Crimes

A discussion of war crimes—and there were crimes on both sides—would require at least one entire book. Hitler's mania for destroying "inferior races," such as gypsies, Jews, and Slavs, led to an appalling number of civilian deaths. Poles, Jews, and other "undesirables" perished by the millions; we would have to return to the campaigns of the medieval Mongols to find like numbers of victims. The horrors of the concentration camps are well known, including the tortures, medical experimentation, and use of human remains.

The Allies were far from blameless. The policy of "strategic" or "terror" bombing sent British and American planes over German cities with orders to bomb, not military targets, but ordinary homes, hospitals, and schools. This was supposed to demoralize the population, possibly on the principle that in a democracy "the people" are responsible for what the government does. The firebombing of Dresden, with the loss of perhaps fifty thousand innocent lives (estimates vary) is one of the worst of the Allied atrocities, but by far not the only one. Such wholesale, deliberate slaughter of civilians can hardly be seen as respecting the principle enunciated by St. Thomas Aquinas that "it is never lawful to kill the innocent."

When the war ended, Operation Keelhaul, one of the provisions of the Yalta Conference, involved repatriating citizens of any Allied country who found themselves outside their homeland at the end of the war. This sounds innocuous, except that it included those who did not want to go: specifically, tens of thousands of non-Communist Ukrainians, Russians, and others who were forcibly returned to Soviet control, where they were summarily shot or thrown into the Gulag.

The bombing of Hiroshima and Nagasaki, which included a large Catholic population, when the Japanese had already tried several times to open peace negotiations, poses a moral dilemma that is difficult to resolve. When I first discussed this issue in print I was inclined to reject the justifications usually made for the use of the atom bomb, on the principle expressed by St. Thomas Aquinas that "it is never lawful to kill the innocent." A thoughtful and informed reader wrote me a letter that made a number of excellent points and led me to do more research on the question. The rationale was that, since the Japanese had rejected unconditional surrender, any other way of ending the war, including invasion of the islands, would have cost many more American lives.

It is also worth mentioning that both Presidents Roosevelt and Truman, who had generally opposed the use of biological warfare or gas, seem to have thought of atomic bombs as simply more powerful versions of traditional explosives. Few if any experts, in fact, seem to have known just what the results on the atom bombs' victims would be.

It now seems that many in the Japanese government and diplomatic corps were in favor of surrender, and proposals were actually submitted to the Soviet representatives at Potsdam. The United States itself had let it be known that the door was open to some sort of peace discussions, although it insisted on the unconditional-surrender part.

One of the sticking points was the Japanese determination to retain the emperor in office along with their traditional form of government. On that, the Americans were willing to allow a postwar Japan eventually to choose its own political system, although the terms were sketchy. The American emphasis, however, was on surrender first. The more intransigent of the Japanese officials dithered over this, with some angling for a peace settlement that was short of surrender, despite the urgent messages they were receiving from their own ambassadors abroad and diplomatic experts at home, strongly advising unconditional surrender. (Gerhard L. Weinberg's massive *A World at Arms, A Global History of World War II* documents the steps in the painful process that brought the most clear-sighted of the Japanese to favor surrender.)

Before the opposing Japanese governmental factions could come to an agreement, American patience with both the dithering and the increasing loss of American lives ran out, and the bomb was dropped on Hiroshima. When surrender was not immediately forthcoming, the same fate befell Nagasaki, with its large Catholic population. I am told that there was an armament factory there, but that did not make accomplices of the numerous civilians, including many children, who were either incinerated or suffered from radiation for the rest of their lives, just as the fact of Japanese soldiers' brutality to their prisoners did not justify the destruction of tens of thousands of civilians who had nothing to do with that. The justification for the bombs must rest on other grounds.

When news of Nagasaki reached the government, still in session to discuss the ins and outs of surrender, the emperor intervened personally and insisted on accepting the American terms. The greatest war in history, at least so far, was over.

Thought and Culture: Prewar and Postwar

A number of developments during the 1920s and 1930s must engage our attention if we are to understand the mentality of the various nations engaged in the Second World War and its aftermath. The first is the growth of the eugenics movement, the second is the spread of Communism, and the third is the role of the Catholic Church during World War II. During this whole period, Sister Lucy of Fatima continued to pass on faithfully the messages of our Lord and our Lady, which received varying responses from the faithful and the papacy.

The Church Under Attack

Euthanasia and Gas Chambers

In the 1920s eugenics was a craze all over the Western world, including in the United States, where some sixty thousand people were forcibly sterilized. An infamous 1924 Supreme Court decision, *Buck v. Bell*, legitimized the process to prevent transmission of supposedly inherited conditions. Chief Justice Oliver Wendell Holmes's famous quip, "Three generations of imbeciles is enough," summed up the mentality of the genetic engineers of the day. The American geneticist Hermann Mueller dreamed of selective breeding and test-tube babies, rhapsodizing, "How many women ... would be eager and proud to rear a child of Lenin or of Darwin!" Admittedly he had peculiar tastes in humans, but Bernard Shaw, C. P. Snow, and Julian Huxley admired him quite a bit.

Then there was birth control, whose goal Margaret Sanger described as "more from the fit, less from the unfit," its purpose being "to create a race of thoroughbreds" and eliminate "human weeds": that "class of humanity who should never have been born at all." Among the "inferior races" that she thought should be sterilized she included "Latins, Slavs, and Hebrews." As for excess babies, she stated, "The most merciful thing a large family can do to one of its infant members is to kill it." Not a nice lady. Phrases such as "absolutely worthless human beings," "foreign body in human society," and "life devoid of value" were current in the writings of the eugenic avant-garde in the 1920s—long before anyone had heard of Hitler.

Meanwhile in Germany during the thirties, *before* Hitler came to power, psychiatrists had begun killing off mental patients with poison gas—an estimated 275,000 of them. To drive home the point that this saved money, 1930s schoolbooks included math problems that required students to figure out how much public housing could be built for the amount of money one insane asylum would cost. Gradually this elimination of patients by doctors was extended to epileptics, people with arteriosclerosis, deaf-mutes, and even the leftover wounded from World War I. The elderly were discreetly targeted. They were interviewed in their homes and then taken away for "evaluation"; when their families asked about them, the families were told they were being institutionalized for a time. In reality, they were being shipped off to gas chambers. Ironically, until late 1940 Jewish psychiatric patients were excluded from the program, apparently because they were undeserving of such compassionate care. (Later they would be particularly targeted.) The accounts of the murders of babies and children—first the mentally ill and the handicapped, later the slow learners and the bed wetters—are the most harrowing; large numbers were starved to death over a period of weeks by the gradual decrease of food. This saved money on both food and death-dealing chemicals. It is interesting to note that the German compulsory sterilization law of 1933 was taken largely from the "Model Eugenic Sterilization Law" composed by an American associate of Margaret Sanger, Harry Laughlin. Another associate who visited Germany in 1940 spoke admiringly of "weeding out the worst strains in the German stock in a scientific and truly humanitarian way."

The Errors of Russia

Meanwhile, the popes had continued to ignore our Lady's request for the consecration of Russia, while the power and influence of the Soviet Union continued to increase. Communist parties were established all over the Western world, and a Communist regime was actually set up in Bavaria following

The Church Under Attack

World War I. Even before Stalin took power in 1928, the many thousands of Russian "enemies of the people" had been exterminated and the first concentration camps set up. During the 1930s, Stalin systematically targeted the kulaks, successful peasant farmers who naturally opposed collectivization of their land. Some seven million of them were shot or died in labor camps. Then it was the turn of Ukraine, where drastically increased food requisitions were used deliberately to produce a famine that took another five million lives. Interestingly, the West remained largely ignorant of this latter atrocity, despite persistent rumors from the Russian borders, because of the constant denials by the *New York Times* correspondent in Moscow, Walter Duranty, that such a thing was taking place. Reports of mass starvation, wrote Duranty, were "bunk." Thanks to his connections and a chummy visit to the White House, Duranty was able to convince President Roosevelt to recognize the Soviet Union.

It was not until 1942, twenty-five years after the Fatima apparitions, that Pope Pius XII consecrated the world to our Lady on October 31, with a veiled reference to Russia. Early in the following year Sister Lucy stated, "The Good God has already shown me His contentment with the act, although incomplete according to His desire, performed by the Holy Father and several bishops. He promises in return to end the war soon. The conversion of Russia is not for now." It still has not happened.

By the 1930s, the errors of Russia were showing up aggressively in Catholic Spain. The Spanish Civil War of 1936–1939 was one of the steps toward World War II in this sense: that the main antagonists took some part in what might have remained a purely domestic Spanish conflict. The republic set up in 1931, following centuries of Catholic monarchy, was neither efficient nor Catholic; in fact, it closed Church-run schools and failed to implement badly needed agrarian reforms. Domestic Communists, with foreign backing as usual, began to foment uprisings, as did socialists and anarchists (who were so violent they attracted professional criminals). General Franco, attempting to restore order and sane government, called for six hundred volunteers to help him; he got forty thousand. Peasants joined him, wearing emblems with "Viva Cristo Rey" on them.

By 1936 both Hitler's Germany and Mussolini's Italy saw the chance to influence a possible strategic ally as well as to test newly developed weapons. They supported Franco's Nationalists. Stalin saw a golden opportunity to establish a Communist state in Spain and sent support for the Communist-influenced republic. (The grateful republic paid him two-thirds of the gold reserves of Spain, before Franco defeated it.) Foreign fellow travelers and mushy-headed liberal idealists such as Hemingway, Orwell, and the Scots Communist Hamish Fraser flocked to Spain to fight for the Communists. Hemingway got a novel out of it: *For Whom the Bell Tolls*. Orwell had the realism to see what was really going on and wrote *Homage to Catalonia*; he became a convinced anti-Stalinist, although with socialist leanings. Fraser, a member of the Soviet secret-police organization in Spain, returned home still a Communist; he became a Catholic some years later and founded the fine traditionalist review *Apropos*. His knowledge of the inner workings of the Communist mind and system made him a valuable opponent of subversion in all its forms.

There is no space here to detail some of the heroic incidents of the war and the martyrdoms of the numerous priests, nuns, and faithful. Franco won, decisively, and brought Spain thirty-six years of peace, during which he laid the ground for Spain's postwar prosperity. Not only did Hitler not get Spanish support in return for the weapons he had sent, since Spain remained neutral, but he could not even obtain access to the Mediterranean or other useful concessions from Franco. After one attempt to extract something useful from him, Hitler was heard to remark, "I would rather have all the teeth in my head pulled than talk to that man again."

The Catholic Church during World War II

To follow the fortunes of the Church in all the major countries throughout the period preceding and during World War II would take volumes. We can mention here only the persecutions in the Soviet Union and in Germany during the war. As early as 1922, a letter from Lenin to the politburo urged the secret police to exploit a famine in the Volga region in order to destroy the Orthodox Church. "Famine," wrote Lenin, "is the only time when we can beat the enemy over the head. Now, when there is cannibalism in famine-stricken areas, we can carry out the expropriation of church valuables with the most furious and ruthless energy.... We must crush their resistance with such cruelty that they will not forget it for decades."

The Church got the message. The following year Patriarch Tikhon stated, "I have completely adopted the Soviet platform and consider that the Church must be nonpolitical." From then on, the Russian Orthodox Church was generally docile to its masters, sometimes to the point of acting as a tool of Soviet policy. This was not necessarily true of individual believers, however, or of the minority Catholics in Russia.

Essential reading for an appreciation of Christian life under Stalin is Father Walter Ciszek's classic account, listed in the reading suggestions.

The Century of Total War: Part Two

The Catholic Church in Germany

It was clear, once the Hitler regime began to show its true colors and develop its neo-pagan ideology, that Nazism was incompatible with Christianity. Many Protestants, including Dietrich Bonhoeffer and Karl Barth, saw this and opposed the regime, but a small group formed the People's Church — a sort of anti-doctrinal, fundamentalist movement that both echoed some of Luther's more radical ideas about the Jews and the German nation and supported the regime's eugenic programs as well as its anti-Semitism. With some six hundred thousand members, they represented a tiny fraction (perhaps 2 percent) of German Protestants, but they were doubtless very useful to the regime.

As for Catholics, it was clear that Nazi principles were incompatible with Church teaching; Catholics were among the most vocal critics of the regime and suffered intense persecution that has been thoroughly documented, even during the first few years of Hitler's rule. The White Rose Resistance, a heroic group of Catholic and other Christian students, led by an Aristotle-quoting Catholic brother and sister, mounted what has been called the only public political display of defiance that occurred in Nazi Germany. It was soon stamped out and its young members executed; the leaders were guillotined.

It is now known that Pope Pius XII was aware of the most significant of the many attempts to assassinate Hitler, led by the Catholic officer Claus von Stauffenberg, and facilitated contact among the parties to the plot — which failed, like all the others. Hitler seems to have had an eerie and uncanny sense of danger and would abruptly alter his schedule or movements for no apparent reason, just when an attempt on his life was to be made. The pope, however, would do much more in the struggle against Hitler, including arranging meetings among foreign secret agents and anti-Nazi Germans to assassinate him, until the pope himself became a Nazi target. In the closing months of the war there were several plans to kidnap the pope (or even assassinate him) and loot the Vatican of its treasures.

Saving the Jews

It is interesting that the word *holocaust* does not appear in older postwar history textbooks; even when it came into use elsewhere, it first referred merely to the total loss of life caused by the Axis powers—the approximately fifty million casualties of World War II. Only later was the word capitalized and used exclusively for the Jews killed by Hitler.

Of most interest to Catholics is the constant repetition of charges against the Church and the papacy for not somehow stopping Hitler or preventing all killing of Jews (the Poles do not blame us for failing to prevent the killing of five to six million Poles). This propaganda assault began only in the 1960s. Immediately after the war, both the Church and the papacy were praised by Jews for their efforts to save them. Israeli historian and diplomat Pinchas Lapide stated that the Catholic Church had saved about 860,000 Jews—more than all the other churches, countries, and relief organizations put together. The chief rabbi of Rome, Rabbi Zolli, was baptized after the war and took the pope's name, Eugenio, as his baptismal name; one cannot imagine a man so dedicated to his people doing that if Pope Pius had really been apathetic about helping the Jews. The story of Rome during the German occupation and the role of the Church in saving not only Allied pilots and soldiers trapped behind enemy lines, but also the Roman Jewish community, is well documented. (Not to be missed is the Gregory

The Century of Total War: Part Two

Peck film *The Scarlet and the Black*, mentioned in the reading suggestions.)

Nevertheless, the appearance of the infamous 1963 play *The Deputy* managed to start the myth of Catholic indifference to the fate of the Jews or even outright collaboration in the Holocaust, with Pope Pius XII as the special target. By 1963, many eyewitnesses who might have contradicted the new myth were dead, and the enemies of the Church were free to churn out attack after attack on the supposed wartime record of the papacy. In recent years the tide of books based on the myth apparently reached its high point; it is gratifying to see that there are now a number of solid refutations of the lies, some of them written by reputable Jews who pay due respect to historical facts. There is still more to be done, of course, and even when the myth has been thoroughly demolished, we can expect it to pursue an underground life like so many other myths, about the Crusades, the Inquisition, the Priory of Zion, the Illuminati, and all the other crazy stuff some of my students just "know" to be true. If this is a depressing note on which to end this period, wait until we get to the postwar era, next chapter.

Chapter 10

Postwar and Post–Cold War

The fragmented world that emerged from World War II and the following period of the Cold War was one of light and shadow. Light and shadow also characterized the pre–Vatican II Church, as the next section will show. Here we will consider the major European states and how they fared in the postwar period.

Postwar France

As the war drew to its end and the desperate Germans took over all of France, Marshal Pétain was taken by force and imprisoned in Germany; he was later liberated by American troops and returned to France, at eighty years old, to the applause of a grateful people, right? Wrong. He was arrested, put on trial for treason, and condemned to life imprisonment in an uncomfortable fortress-prison. General de Gaulle had entered Paris with his supporters and, for want of anybody else to take charge, became head of state; he appointed the head of the Communist Party, Maurice Thorez, as his lieutenant (Thorez had defected to Moscow while Hitler and Stalin were still allies—making him a traitor, but that didn't seem to bother anybody in the new regime.) This is called the Liberation. It was really a replay of the French Revolution, for the fourth or fifth time in French history. The Resistance men came out of their tunnels and began to settle old political scores. Anyone who got in their left-wing way was labeled a collaborator, hunted down, and either killed quickly or tortured to death. Only some were actually German collaborators. The death toll rivaled that of the French Revolution and exceeded that of the Commune of 1870–1871: 80,000 by an American estimate, 105,000 according to a later French estimate. People were in fear of their lives for years after the war. A French Catholic nurse who had been part of the Resistance and had been given the Legion of Honor medal learned many years later what the Resistance had really done and sent back the medal. This is a period with which France has still not come to terms. It remains a sore point and a source of division, like the French Revolution itself.

Decolonization

England found itself in a position it had not been in for centuries: from being one of the greatest imperial powers, it soon turned into an empire with only a few shreds of colonies left, and the same fate befell the other colonial powers. Subjects of the European colonies in Asia and elsewhere had been much impressed with the initial successes of Japan, a nonwestern power, in defeating previously invincible European forces. Japan thus appeared as a liberator of the Eastern colonies of Britain, France, the Netherlands, and so forth, and enthusiasm for freedom from colonial rule spread, fueled by the Enlightenment ideologies of democracy and the rights of man purveyed by the colonizers themselves. Principally during the 1940s and 1950s, but continuing into the '80s, virtually all the European colonial empires collapsed, with sometimes tragic consequences. There were some success stories, but in many places—Algeria, Afghanistan, Israel, much of southeastern Africa—the violence has never completely stopped. Miserable economies, political corruption (with the West insisting on democracy in places such as Rwanda, where it did not fit and did not work), and increasing tribalism and territorial fragmentation continue to plague the former colonies. The flood of immigrants into the former imperial countries has swamped social services and turned whole cities in England and France into immigrant enclaves, with chronic instability as the result.

The Former Enemy Powers

In the long run, both Germany and Japan, largely with American aid and support, again became economic powerhouses and world powers. In the long run however, as John Maynard Keynes remarked, "we are all dead." The Germans and Japanese were not all dead, of course, but hundreds of thousands of them were; in the case of Japan, we had seen to that with our atom bombs. As for Germany, which concerns us here, the end of the war was appalling. The Russians, invading Germany from the east, took a grim revenge with mass atrocities and slaughter. At the Potsdam Conference in July and August of 1945, considered the beginning of the Cold War, Truman and Churchill continued the policy previously adopted at Yalta that had placed Eastern Europe within the Soviet sphere of influence. Specifically, they agreed at Potsdam to allow the removal of millions of Germans from Eastern European territories in which many German families had lived for centuries. Both Russians and the puppet regimes they had installed in the countries within "their" sphere took part. Some twelve million or more Germans were forcibly driven out of their homes in 1945 and

1946, in the greatest migration Europe had ever seen. Herded into camps, they were at the mercy of their captors; brutalized and tortured, German men, women, and children died by the tens of thousands. German women were crucified on the sides of barns or thrown off bridges, and refugee ships in the Baltic were sunk by Soviet planes. The British Jewish writer Victor Gollancz stated that the Allies were treating these civilians as the Jews had been treated by Himmler.

The Fate of Germany

The Allies had agreed to keep Germany weak and let it get along as well as it could after the war. By the winter of 1945, however, starvation and disease were threatening the surviving Germans. The United States and Great Britain began to supply food and reconsider their relationship with the defeated enemy state.

The country was divided into four zones—French, British, American, and Russian—with the capital, Berlin, similarly divided. Berlin, however, was located within the Russian zone, which precipitated one of the first crises of the Cold War, a term that refers to the state of often extreme hostility, just short of actual warfare, between the West and the Soviet Union. Each occupying nation was to prepare its zone for inclusion in a new all-German government. France initially balked at this for various reasons we need not go into; the point is that this gave the Soviet Union an excuse to drag its feet also. Indeed, it soon set up a Communist government within its zone and began to confiscate and dismantle German factories and ship the parts to Russia. Meanwhile, the American and British zones were mostly fused into what would become—when the French finally cooperated—West Germany.

Postwar and Post–Cold War

The winter of 1946–1947 was unusually severe, and only the United States was capable of providing the massive aid Germany required. The Marshall Plan of 1947 offered aid to any European country that would reveal its economic situation and the degree to which it could cooperate in its own recovery. The Soviet Union would not participate; it was unwilling to reveal its economic situation or any other information and would not allow its satellites to do so, so eastern European postwar recovery would be painfully slow. The following year, the USSR walked out of the four-power council for Germany and blocked Western access to Berlin. If the Western powers did nothing, the whole city would come under Soviet control; on the other hand, they feared that forcing their way across the Soviet zone to reach the Western parts of Berlin might provoke war. (It is worth recalling that the West could have taken Berlin during the last days of the war and avoided this whole problem, but it apparently lacked the will.)

The Berlin Airlift

In an ingenious and heroic episode of the early Cold War, American and British planes began to supply the Western zones of Berlin. Everything—from paperclips to food to fuel—had to come by plane. American planes were making 250 deliveries a day (2,500 tons of supplies) in July 1948. By the following spring, planes were landing every two minutes, delivering 8,000 tons a day. Some planes and pilots were lost, but the West showed no sign of giving up the project. One pilot described how friends began to give him packets of toys to drop for the children, and this became a regular feature of his flights. He noticed, however, as he neared the border with the Soviet zone, that children were gathering on the other side and wistfully watching the toys fall out of their reach. The pilot began making quick and risky detours over the border so that those children would have toys too. In May 1949, the Soviet Union gave in and lifted the blockade; in the same month, the Federal Republic of Germany was founded in the west of the country, while the Soviet Union set up the satellite state of East Germany.

Counterrevolutions

It was ruthless Communist ideologues, not the Russian people, who had made the great revolution of the twentieth century, as French ideologues had made the French Revolution. In both cases, "the people" were persecuted for their attachment to their churches and monarchs — Louis XVI and Louis XVII in France, Czar Nicholas in Russia. Both countries, and the revolutionary empires they acquired, saw the rise of counterrevolutionary movements that eventually produced major regime change. For Russia and Eastern Europe, that change was agonizingly slow in coming. The first major postwar outbreaks of counterrevolution began in the mid-1950s. The death of Stalin in 1953 was followed by a speech by Khrushchev that dared to question parts of the Stalinist legend previously imposed. Soon there were outbreaks of counterrevolutionary activity in East Germany, Poland, Czechoslovakia, and the Soviet Union itself. The most harrowing was the Hungarian counterrevolution of 1956.

S.O.S. — Save Our Souls

That was one of the desperate radio messages sent by the young leaders of the attempt to overthrow Soviet rule in Hungary in the last days of that tragic fight. The West already knew the character of the Hungarian Communist regime from the public trial of Cardinal Mindszenty, primate of Hungary and—in the Hungarian political tradition—regent of the country in the absence of a legitimate government. (See the following section for the story of the cardinal and the Communist show trial.) In October 1956, what had begun as a student gathering at the statue of a famous Hungarian poet to read his patriotic poetry aloud turned into a mass demonstration against the regime. As the resistance escalated, the occupying Soviet troops, taken by surprise, pulled back to their barracks and to the eastern part of the country. Relying on encouragements to revolt that had long been broadcast from the West, including the Voice of America, the demonstrators expected Western help and recognition for the new government they began to set up. They liberated Cardinal Mindszenty from captivity, and the whole country was behind the movement to reestablish a free Hungary.

Days went by, however, with nothing but silence from the Western powers, including the United States. President Eisenhower had just had a heart attack, and Great Britain and France were involved in a standoff with Egypt over the closing of the Suez Canal. None of them had time for Hungary. Realizing this, the Soviet troops moved back in, this time to suppress the freedom fighters; the photographs of children throwing stones and Molotov cocktails at the Russian tanks in the streets of Budapest are well known. (Many of the children were rounded up and taken to prison in the Soviet Union. According to some Hungarian sources, the Russians kept them in jail until they were twenty-one; then they took them out and shot them.) It soon became evident that further resistance was hopeless, and hundreds of thousands of Hungarians fled the country. For those who remained, the future was bleak, although the Soviets sought to placate them with a certain degree of liberalization in the reimposed dictatorship; perhaps, they seem to have thought, the slaves could be distracted with a measured dose of consumerism.

Berlin Again

By 1960, one-sixth of the population of East Germany, most of them young professionals and skilled workers, had "gone west"—they had simply crossed the border that divided East and West Germany. When, in 1961, the movement west had become almost a stampede, with thousands leaving over a single weekend, the authorities began to build a wall to divide the city. They began cautiously, to test the West's reaction; there was none, so the building continued. (A witness to Warsaw Pact discussions on the subject later testified that Khrushchev was prepared to make the East Germans stop the project if the Western powers tore down the first part of the wall. Of course that didn't happen.) The wall did not stop the seepage of German citizens heading for freedom, but it made the enterprise far more hazardous, as numerous photographs of individuals and families shot down by snipers on the wall attest.

The Collapse

It was not until the late eighties, during the reign of Gorbachev in the Soviet Union, that widespread protests again developed; all over the Soviet bloc, television viewers became aware that people in neighboring states were resisting Communist tyranny, and they flocked into the streets to do the same. (This recalls the spread of the revolutions of 1830 and 1848, when demonstrations in one state sparked others.) The Communist system imploded at last: in November 1989, the Berlin border was opened and the wall torn down. The ongoing problems of the former Soviet satellites are beyond the scope of this brief survey, but at least they were freed of foreign tyranny. The collapse of the Soviet Union also left the United States as the world's only global superpower. What comes next is in the works now, although we do not see it very clearly.

Catholic Thought and Culture in the Mid-Twentieth Century

The Church had many reasons for rejoicing and for grieving during the Cold War. In the West, peace allowed for the resumption of her ordinary life and activities, and vocations were not lacking. New ideas, however, were beginning to influence Catholics in many areas, and not all of them were good. In the eastern part of Europe, on the other hand, as well as in China and other areas in the process of falling to Communist conquest, the persecution of Catholics rivaled or exceeded that of the Roman period. The Church was struck a greater blow than anyone realized when Pope Pius XII — intelligent, learned, courageous, and a great defender of orthodoxy — died. The pontificate of John XXIII, forecast at the time to be a brief period of transition, marked a turning point for the Church: it would be John XXIII who would call the Second Vatican Council.

The Church in the West

During the immediate postwar period and throughout the 1950s, the Church in the United States experienced a golden age. Large numbers of converts were welcomed by increasing numbers of priests, nuns, and religious; children were taught almost exclusively by nuns in Catholic schools, and patients of Catholic hospitals were nursed by sisters. The beautiful Tridentine liturgy was generally celebrated piously, congregations dressed for the occasion, and even non-Catholic businesses closed on Sundays and between 12 and 3 on Good Friday. That was when Catholics crowded churches for three hours of solemn devotion and sermons on the Seven Last Words of Our Lord. Bishop Fulton Sheen's television talks were enormously popular, and Catholics were taken seriously. Catholic movie actresses such as Ann Blyth promoted modest dress designs that carried "Marylike" tags in the department stores. Catholic boycotts of indecent films caused theaters to stop showing them.

The European Catholic Scene

All this may sound like fantasy, but it is not, as anyone who lived in those days knows. Things were somewhat different, however, in Europe. In France, ever the source of new thinking, for good or for ill, many new ideas were percolating. The increase in domestic Communists sparked an interest in Marxism within the French Church, from a desire to refute it or to incorporate it into Catholic thinking. The Marxist emphasis on work and action as the main concerns of life promoted a worldly and activist mentality at odds with traditional Catholic thought. In response to this new trend, Josef Pieper wrote his little gem of a book called *Leisure: The Basis of Culture*. In it he championed the classical principle that work was not the whole of life, as in Marxist and Calvinist thinking. Rather, we work in order to have leisure, and the highest activity of leisure is contemplation. (In our present frenetic world in which time is taken up with constant multitasking and worthless "entertainment," this book should be required reading for serious Catholics at least once a year.)

Atheist philosophers such as Jean-Paul Sartre came up with the dour system called Existentialism, which posits that we have no fixed essence but rather create ourselves by our choices; its creator's view that "Hell is other people" gives an idea of its dismal character. Some Catholic philosophers such as Gabriel Marcel, however, tried to develop a Christian approach to the philosophical problem of existence, which had so intrigued St. Thomas before his death. One hears little of this school of thought now, perhaps because it was succeeded by phenomenology, which had first been developed by agnostic German thinkers and then elaborated by Catholic thinkers, as Marcel had done with Existentialism. I say nothing of the merits of these new systems, finding them enormously abstruse compared with the clarity of Aristotle and Aquinas, but that may be ignorance on my part. The point is that they represent intellectual novelties, and in that they are part of the general movement in every area that began to build up after the war. If there were new schools of philosophy, why not of theology? If some changes had been made in the liturgy by Pope Pius XII, such as the restoration of the ancient Easter vigil, why not more? Why not learn more about what the early Church did and copy that, or else create new forms more in tune with the modern age? Combining the Marxist emphasis on the plight of the workers — which was actually a serious problem — with a desire for changes in traditional missionary methods, the worker-priests threw themselves into the world of work to such a degree that many ended up leaving the priesthood. Change is what they were calling for, and the change zealots would not have long to wait. By the time the council opened, Modernists were resurfacing from the underground existence they had been leading since their condemnation by St. Pius X, and progressives of all stripes were joining them. What in the previous century had been called the heresy of Americanism began oozing back into the intellectual life of American Catholic thinkers, reinforcing European progressive ideology. The stage was set for Vatican II.

Communist Europe

There was no such progressivism in Eastern Europe, where persecution reinforced Catholic determination to maintain the traditional Faith in all its purity in harsh circumstances. In the Soviet satellites, deviation from orthodoxy was more likely to be expressed in attempts to compromise with Communist ideology and policies: the "peace priests" who surfaced in the various countries of the Eastern bloc were one example. The Communist authorities knew that in order to control the minds of their largely Catholic populations, they had to control the Church. They could strangle her operations with impossible regulations, but that did not destroy the religion itself. They therefore adopted a policy of infiltrating agents into the Church, including the seminaries, with a mission to bore from within. In other cases, the authorities were able to persuade priests to cooperate with them. These peace priests were willing to compromise with the Soviet system, either from opportunism, genuine sympathy for Communism, the idea that otherwise their flocks would be even more bereft, or other reasons. These collaborators existed at all levels of Church structure, and the faithful distrusted them and avoided confessing to them.

The clerical heroes of the Eastern bloc, including the Soviet Union and the satellites, were numerous, many of them still unknown, except to those closest to them. Some outstanding cardinals such as the Polish Cardinal Wyszynski and Yugoslav Archbishop Stepinac stood up publicly to the oppressors; perhaps the best known of these martyrs is Cardinal Mindszenty, prince-primate of Hungary. As a humble parish priest he had been imprisoned under the brief Communist regime of 1919 in Hungary and then again because of his opposition to the Germans in 1944. During the postwar period he worked tirelessly to rebuild both the country and the Faith, inspiring the faithful and organizing food distribution to the needy. He became so popular, and so uncompromising in his orthodoxy, that the Communists viewed him as a major threat to their control and decided to eliminate him. Charged, ludicrously, with black marketeering and other crimes, he was imprisoned in 1948, tortured repeatedly, and put on public trial. He had stated in advance that any confession he made would be forced and therefore invalid. It is clear from the film footage of his courtroom appearances that he was not himself, and he later described how he had been drugged. Innocuous statements were read to him that he was asked to sign; damning admissions were deftly substituted, however, when the papers were placed before him for quick signatures. On the basis of such fraudulent maneuvers, the cardinal was condemned to death—a sentence that was magnanimously commuted to life in prison. Making an example of such a man backfired on the regime, and Cardinal Mindszenty, even during his years of imprisonment, was not forgotten by his countrymen. Liberated during the 1956 counter-revolution, he became once again a rallying point for Catholic Hungary, until the Soviet repression forced him into sanctuary in the American Embassy.

He was, incredibly, forced to leave that refuge by Pope Paul VI in 1971, after refusing to resign as primate of Hungary. In 1973, the pope stripped the cardinal of his titles and declared the position of primate vacant. Mindszenty issued a statement declaring that he had not resigned. He settled in Austria and from there he traveled the world, encouraging Hungarian

Catholics to be faithful to their religion, even in exile. Following Mindszenty's death in 1975, Pope Paul appointed in his place another, more pliant, cardinal who got along quite well with the Communist authorities. It was not until years after his death that his body was finally returned to his native land, where it now rests in the great episcopal cathedral of Esztergom, near a new museum dedicated to the life and work of this great Catholic hero.

The Rome-Moscow Agreement

Why did the Church treat him this way? Why, for that matter, did the Church mute her former militant criticisms of Communism following the death of Pius XII? Why did the council say nothing about the plight of millions of Catholics under Communist oppression all over the world? Why was the occasion not taken to consecrate Russia to our Lady under the conditions she specified to Sister Lucy? What business could possibly have been more important or more urgent?

Not long after the council, some partial explanations emerged. The Vatican had for years been pursuing a policy of rapport with the Soviet Union in hope that conditions might be improved for the Church in the captive nations if only it were sufficiently conciliatory. (It may be added here that some such cautious, conciliatory policies had always had a place in the Church, beginning with her dealings with the Roman imperial authorities. I believe it was Stalin who asked, contemptuously, how many armored divisions the Church had. Having none, she has always had to do what she could for her flock in times of persecution—which often amounted to very little.) According to some accounts the Vatican, in 1961 and 1962, reassured the representatives of the Russian Orthodox Church that the Soviet Communist regime would not be attacked at the council, saying that the council would be "nonpolitical." For what turned out to be an illusory rapprochement, Cardinal Mindszenty was sacrificed and the consecration of Russia by the council did not take place.

Eventually, of course, the Soviet empire collapsed and the former satellites were free once again. Once the walls and curtains came down, however, the council had happened. The old, faithful priests released from Communist prisons or internal exile returned, thinking to rebuild the Faith of their people and celebrate the rites of the Church freely once again. Instead, they were propagandized by zealous missionaries of Vatican II and all the new thinking that came with it—or after it, for the council was not responsible for all the Modernist ideas that proliferated among the liberal clergy. Western Jesuits meeting shortly after the fall of Communism in Eastern Europe to discuss "helping" the Church there were quoted as declaring that they had to "update those people."

Here, for those who did not live through the "updating" period, we should mention the wave of "experimentation," particularly liturgical experimentation, that afflicted the Church in the years following the "updating" of the Mass. Where religious progressives abounded, particularly in parts of the United States, the updating often assumed odd forms—sometimes to the point of sacrilege. Clown Masses, dancing girls in the sanctuary, and other abuses spread. A parish not far from Washington, DC, had a particularly colorful pastor who enjoyed entering the sanctuary for Christmas Midnight Mass dressed as a Christmas tree with flashing lights. Another time he arrived at the altar by way of a Volkswagen that he drove down the center aisle. (One hopes that some degree of insanity mitigated his responsibility for all this.) He seemed to get away with it for quite a while.

No wonder Mass attendance fell and serious Catholics searched frantically for legitimate traditional Masses (which had been banned, with only a few exceptions allowed) or changed over to an Eastern rite. Now imagine the impact of all this updating suddenly imposed on the former Communist states of Eastern Europe, where all the clandestine Masses said by all the martyrs for several decades had been the Mass of all time. The use of the vernacular, the new rites of the Mass and the sacraments, and the "new theology" were all bewildering—at least in the short term—to those who had held on so long to the religion of pre-Communist days.

Postconciliar Religious Education

New theological approaches also trickled down, in the 1960s and 1970s, to the level of religious education. One director of religious education tried to disabuse me of my outdated belief in angels. I asked her what our Lord meant when he referred to the little children "whose angels see God." She gave me a pitying smile and explained carefully that we used to think the word *angel* meant "spirit," but now we know it just meant "a messenger." Oh. A friend was told that purgatory doesn't exist because "Jesus wouldn't do things that way."

Things really do seem to be better now, however, on many other fronts. The recent liturgical changes to the Mass prayers restore some of them to their ancient forms; the Tridentine Mass seems to be far more widely available now than at any time since the council. There seem to be far fewer liberals among recent seminary graduates and more priests with solid theological backgrounds. We have a number of thoroughly orthodox religious orders and colleges and many educated, intelligent, and articulate lay speakers and writers who do a great deal in educating the laity.

And What of Our Lady?

The immediate postwar period was one of triumph for Our Lady of Fatima. Devotion to her had been widespread and fervent during the war, from the highest levels of the hierarchy to the ordinary faithful. Beginning with tours around Portugal starting in 1946, when the "miracle of the doves" first occurred—the phenomenon of doves nestling at the feet of the statue and accompanying it on its journey—the travels of our Lady's statue throughout Western Europe, and later the world, drew large and enthusiastic throngs eager to do her honor and entreat her help. In those days, bishops welcomed her arrival, crowned her, and encouraged the Fatima devotions and prayers for the conversion of Russia. Today the Pilgrim Virgin statues still circulate, but few are the churches with First Saturday devotions and the prayers dictated to the children by the angel and Our Lady at Fatima, unfamiliar to most Catholics now since they are never mentioned by Rome or from the pulpit. Unsurprisingly, Russia is not converted either.

Conclusion

What can we say about the state of the Church in the twenty-first century? What has become of the many questions we have discussed in this brief historical survey? Since we cannot deal with all of them here, we might look at those that caused the greatest problems for the Church in modern times.

When we started our look at the Church's journey through the modern period, the Reformation was shattering Catholic unity and bringing religious war as well as new religions. Protestant-Catholic wars have largely ceased (except perhaps in Northern Ireland), but those new religions have certainly not gone away. The vitality of most of them, however, seems greatly diminished. The contemporary Protestant threat seems to come more from the newer, "charismatic" sects zealously proselytizing in traditional Catholic countries, particularly in Latin America but also in the United States.

In the sixteenth and seventeenth centuries, Islam had become a significant threat when it launched major military attacks on Europe and the Mediterranean. No one would say that that threat is absent today, as Islamic proselytizing and terrorist action have spread throughout much of the world. Islam seems today, as it was then, almost completely impervious to proselytism.

We saw appalling persecution of Catholics in the course of our survey, not just in the Reformation period but in most of the centuries we covered. The French revolutionaries persecuted the Church, as did the revolutionaries in much of Europe, including Nazi Germany and Soviet Russia. Persecution has by no means disappeared in the twenty-first century, but it is less visible to us since it is taking place in China and other parts of Asia, and in Africa. Because of the lack of news coverage, we are often unaware of the many martyrs the Church is still counting.

Major heresies were dealt with at the time of the Reformation by the Council of Trent, but the modern period has seen the rise of that stubborn and slippery "compendium of all heresies" known as Modernism. In one form or another it continues to infect today's Church; when you read about some recalcitrant theologian espousing "doctrinal evolution" or similar notions, you can bet he is a stubborn old Modernist trying once more to "update" Catholic doctrine.

In other words, some of the old ills are with us still. What about the bright side? One good sign of our times would seem to be the rise of new and dynamic religious orders and institutes dedicated to doctrinal and liturgical purity: the Institute of Christ the King and the Priestly Fraternity of St. Peter are two such orders, but there are many more new monastic foundations, orders of nuns, and other organisms—both here and abroad—that have arisen to espouse the cause of orthodoxy, as well as the Catholic cultural and intellectual heritage.

The increasing availability and popularity of the traditional Mass is another good sign; the old Latin Mass brings with it a

Conclusion

whole history and heritage of Catholic culture, decorum, and reverence. It is the rite that formed practically all the saints in the calendar and will continue to do so as it spreads throughout the Church. Lastly, one might point to the hopeful sign of new Catholic colleges and educational institutes dedicated to orthodox teaching and the moral and cultural formation of new generations of Catholics. In the United States there are several of these, perhaps more than in the rest of Christendom.

After all the Church has suffered over the last few unpleasant centuries, then, she has not only survived but managed to flourish—as she will continue to do until the end of time. The Church, after all, is Christ in the world, and he will not be vanquished.

Suggestions for Further Reading

Chapter 1: The Busy Sixteenth Century

The Reformation is an enormous topic, sprawling all over the European continent and affecting theology, economics, politics, culture, and many other facets of life. Warren Carroll's *The Cleaving of Christendom* (Front Royal, Virginia: Christendom Press, 2000) is a good recent summary of the topic from a Catholic perspective.

An excellent study by a non-Catholic that explodes many of the myths about the Reformation, as well as describing how and why it got off the ground, is *The European Reformation*, by Euan Cameron (Oxford: Clarendon Press, 1991).

Sometimes novels, provided they are written by thoroughly knowledgeable authors, can provide us with a vivid glimpse of a historical period from the inside, in a way that ordinary history cannot. For the Reformation, particularly in England, there are a number of first-rate novels by Msgr. Robert Hugh Benson that I cannot recommend too highly. Before reading them it would be a good idea to read a summary of the English Reformation, whether in a book or in an online *Catholic Encyclopedia* article, and note the dates of the monarchs from Henry VIII through Charles II; this is not essential, but it adds to the enjoyment of the story. Msgr. Benson, a convert to Catholicism, was the son of an Anglican archbishop of Canterbury and was thus in a position to know the religious mentality and psychology of both the Protestants and Catholics who appear in his stories. Many of his characters are historical persons, some of them saints. It is worth reading the novels in chronological order, if possible, because some characters turn up in more than one story. *The King's Achievement* deals with life under Henry VIII; *The Queen's Tragedy* (which seems to me the least successful work) describes the reign of Mary Tudor; *Come Rack, Come Rope* takes place under Elizabeth. Unfortunately the edition most widely available is a condensed version; try to get the entire work. It includes St. Edmund Campion as a character. *By What Authority* deals with the later years of the reign of Elizabeth, and *Oddsfish* is set in the reign of Charles II and movingly presents Charles's embrace of the Catholic Faith and reception of the sacraments in his final moments.

Several of the works listed in chapter 1, such as Eamon Duffy's *Stripping of the Altars* (New Haven, Connecticut: Yale University Press, 1992, 2005) will also serve for facts about the Counter-Reformation.

It is impossible to list all the good biographies of, or writings by, the Counter-Reformation saints; to enumerate even the ones in my own library would take too much space. The best practice might be to read the online *Catholic Encyclopedia* entry for a saint in whom you are interested and note the biographies mentioned. Because that edition of the *Catholic Encyclopedia* dates from the early twentieth century, its references include very old books, yet some are extremely interesting and worth reading. One appealing example of an older work is *Saint Philip Neri, Apostle of Rome,* by Cardinal Alfonso Capecelatro (London: Burns, Oates and Washbourne, Ltd., 1926). Another is Margaret Yeo's *The Greatest of the Borgias* (on St. Francis Borgia), written in the style of a historical novel, although it is grounded in historical sources. It was originally published in 1936 but has been reprinted several times.

The fierce persecutions in England and the heroic attempts of Catholics to persevere in trying to win back their country to the Faith have been chronicled in a vast number of sources. There have been several recent works on St. Thomas More, of varying quality, but the two film versions of *A Man for All Seasons* are also still worth viewing. The complex character of Henry VIII is fascinating to watch on the screen, as are a number of the minor characters. *The Autobiography of a Hunted Priest,* by John Gerard, published in several editions, is a chilling eyewitness account of the adventures of a Jesuit priest in England in the early seventeenth century, at the time of the Gunpowder Plot (in which Catholics were charged with attempting to blow up King James I and Parliament, a rather obscure plot that served as a pretext for a vicious crackdown on Catholics in general). Fr. Gerard survived this period of persecution and was able to leave England; others were not so fortunate, as the book describes. A very fine and well-illustrated work on the Gunpowder Plot is Antonia Fraser's *Faith and Treason* (New York: Doubleday, 1996). Lady Antonia has the gift of sympathy for the historical figures she studies so thoroughly as well as the novelist's gift for interesting writing. (Fr. Gerard, the author of *The Autobiography of a Hunted Priest,* is discussed in this work as well.) Antonia Fraser's exhaustive biography of Mary Queen of Scots, who was executed by Queen Elizabeth, is also an outstanding work.

The Church Under Attack

Warren Carroll's *The Cleaving of Christendom* is useful for the topics discussed in the latter part of chapter 1. *A Handbook on Guadalupe* (New Bedford, Massachusetts: Franciscan Friars of the Immaculate, 1997) is an excellent collection of essays on the image of Our Lady of Guadalupe and its Mexican context, with mention of the copy of the image that sailed against the Turks. My *Islam at the Gates* (Manchester, New Hampshire: Sophia Institute Press, 2008) deals with the whole period of the Turkish Wars, as well as the major battles and leaders on both sides. There are also many websites dealing with the wars against the Turks and specific battles, such as Lepanto, that are well worth browsing.

Chapter 2: The Seventeenth Century

The works suggested for chapter 1 are also useful for the topics treated in this one. For Ireland, an older, but extremely readable work is *The Story of the Irish Race: A Popular History of Ireland*, by Seumas MacManus and other Irish scholars. It was written in 1931, revised, and reprinted several times. The brief account Charles II wrote of some of his adventures was published as *King Charles Preserved* (London: The Rodale Press, 1956). A biography of St. Claude is *Perfect Friend: The Life of Blessed Claude la Colombière, S.J.*, by Georges Guitton, S.J. (St. Louis, Missouri, and London: B. Herder Book Company, 1956).

There are numerous fine works on seventeenth-century England, of which only a few can be mentioned here. On the reign of Charles I, C.V. Wedgwood has written a fine trio: *The King's Peace*, *The King's War*, and an account of his trial and execution, *A Coffin for King Charles*. Hugh Ross Williamson, in a short work dedicated to Miss Wedgwood, describes the king's last day: *The Day They Killed the King*. For Charles II, a distressing blend of dash, libertinage, and faith, Msgr. Robert Hugh Benson's *Oddsfish*, an exciting historical novel, gives a fine view of the man and his time. A very fine historian of this period, author of a number of excellent and objective studies, is Antonia Fraser. Besides her biography of James I and her outstanding account of his mother, Mary Queen of Scots, she has produced a marvelously sympathetic account of the Gunpowder Plot entitled *Faith and Treason*. Her Cromwell may be the best biography of this strange man.

Louis XIII, the Just, by A. Lloyd Moote (Berkeley, California: University of California Press, 1989; paperback reprint 1991) is a revisionist treatment of Louis, bringing him out of the shadow of his domineering minister and revealing his own character and personality.

Hilaire Belloc's *Richelieu* is perhaps the most readable of the dozens—perhaps hundreds—of biographies of this powerful character.

The Thirty Years' War, by C. V. Wedgwood, first published in 1956 and since reprinted, is somewhat dated but, like all Miss Wedgwood's books, is very readable. Her final remarks about Innocent X's condemnation of the peace treaty seem somewhat inaccurate; in a papal brief, the pope expressed forcefully his dissatisfaction with a number of provisions unfavorable to the Church, but certainly did not "solemnly" condemn it. (The statement that he issued a papal bull doing so, as stated by some writers, is erroneous.)

There are numerous works on all aspects of the seventeenth-century Ottoman-Christian campaigns, including individual battles and biographies of the major characters involved. The books I have used, such as various volumes of Pastor's monumental *History of the Popes*; *The New Cambridge Modern History*;

and *A Thousand Years of Christianity in Hungary* (a fine historical work that accompanied a museum exhibit in Hungary but is difficult to obtain here) are accessible only through some libraries. My *Islam at the Gates* is also useful for this period.

The following website, while not a scholarly one, has a good summary of the events discussed in this chapter, as well as many fine photographs and artifacts related to the period: http://www.romeartlover.it/Vieturch.html.

There is a famous Hungarian historical novel about the legendary Turkish siege of the city of Eger in 1552, which has appeared in an English translation as *Eclipse of the Crescent Moon*, written by Géza Gárdony, translated by George F. Cushing (Budapest: Corvina Books, 1997). The author did extensive research on the famous siege, reading the sources in several languages and consulting the Ottoman archives. The result is a thrilling story and what seems an authentic picture of life in Hungary under Turkish occupation.

A vast literature is available for the Catholic heroes of this period, including many good translations of writings of the saints. A good introduction to the Catholic culture of the time can be found in both volumes of *The Church in the Seventeenth Century*, by Henri Daniel-Rops; they are part of his multivolume *History of the Church of Christ* and exist in many editions. On the saints, there are far too many books to list; older, scholarly works are often—although not always—better than very recent works. For St. Vincent de Paul, Daniel-Rops's *Monsieur Vincent* is well known, and Mary Purcell's *The World of Monsieur Vincent* (New York: Charles Scribner's Sons, 1963) situates him in the context of his time. The standard scholarly work is *The Life and Works of Saint Vincent de Paul*, by Pierre Coste, C.M., published in 1934; it has been translated by Joseph Leonard,

Suggestions for Further Reading

C.M., and published in three volumes by The Newman Press in 1952. Marie Cecilia Buehrle's *Kateri of the Mohawks*, which I first distrusted for its novelistic style, turned out to be a little gem, bringing to life the Indian world of Kateri and her missionary saviors. A more scholarly treatment of the period immediately preceding the lifetime of Kateri is *Saint Among the Hurons: The Life of Jean de Brébeuf*, by Francis X. Talbot, S.J. (Both these works exist in hardcover and paperback editions.) For St. John Eudes, one can't do better than read what he himself had to say, and several of his works are available in translation. *The Life and the Kingdom of Jesus in Christian Souls: A Treatise on Christian Perfection for Use by Clergy and Laity* (New York: P. J. Kennedy & Sons, 1946) has an introduction by Fulton J. Sheen. Finally, in addition to the biography of St. Claude de la Colombière by Georges Guitton, listed earlier, the saint's spiritual retreats, letters, and treatises are widely available in translation. One such book is *Faithful Servant: Spiritual Retreats and Letters of Blessed Claude La Colombière* (St. Louis, Missouri, and London: B. Herder Book Company, 1960). Margaret Yeo's *These Three Hearts* is a popular study of the relationship between St. Claude, St. Margaret Mary, and of course, the Sacred Heart. The writings of St. Margaret Mary are also well worth tracking down.

There are too many fine articles on the Galileo case to mention here. A very good research paper for the Catholic League by Robert P. Lockwood is available at http://www.catholicleague.org under "Archives," "Research Papers".

Tom Bethell's *Politically Incorrect Guide to Science* (Washington, DC: Regnery, 2005) includes a good summary of the Galileo case. *Galileo, Science and the Church*, by Jerome J. Langford (Ann Arbor, Michigan: University of Michigan Press, 1971;

expanded and updated in the third edition, 1992) is a useful exploration of various theories about the case from many angles and is helpful for those seriously interested in the many details and broad context of the affair. *Galileo's Daughter*, by Dava Sobel (paperback edition by Penguin Books, New York, 2000) is a charming account of Sister Maria Celeste, devoted daughter of a difficult father, and her touching relationship with him. The many quotations from her letters reveal her personality and the issues with which she had to deal in watching over the aging Galileo.

Chapter 3: The Eighteenth Century

It is hard to find one book that gives an adequate presentation of Europe—along with its increasingly important colonies—in the eighteenth century. Perhaps Henri Daniel-Rops's *The Church in the Eighteenth Century* is the place to start. He surveys the intellectual revolution (the Enlightenment), deism, the dynamism of Catholic missionary work, the tragic suppression of the Jesuits, and the interplay of national and papal politics. He also discusses the saints of the period, although there were fewer—in France at least—than in earlier times, probably due to the corrosive intellectual climate and worldliness. An older work by a Catholic historian that presents a clearly organized overview of the eighteenth century in the context of what preceded and followed it is *A Political and Social History of Modern Europe*, by Carlton Hayes (several editions). The first volume begins with the sixteenth century and goes through the eighteenth; while much of it is outdated and the whole necessarily condensed, it is worth reading as a fairly straight path through a maze of complex events. Biographies of some of the major figures of the time, including massive ones of Peter the

Great and Frederick II, abound and dwell upon all the seamy details. It is refreshing to read the story of Maria Theresa as told by the English writer Edward Crankshaw (*Maria Theresa* [New York: The Viking Press, 1970]). He may be neither Catholic nor a professional historian, but he does a wonderful job of bringing to life the Catholic empress and her era.

Works written specifically on the Enlightenment tend to be somewhat technical philosophically and not well suited to the general reader. There are a number of works on Liberalism and other aspects of Enlightenment thought that make for easier reading and will be mentioned in later chapters. For the philosophy student, there is no substitute for reading the original texts of Descartes, the British Empiricists (Locke, Berkeley, Hume), Rousseau, and the rest of the gang. The fourth, fifth, and sixth volumes of Father Frederick Copleston's *History of Philosophy* present a thorough survey of Enlightenment thought. On the political ferment spawned by the Enlightenment in both France and the British American colonies, an excellent study is *The Revolutionary Spirit in France and America*, by Bernard Fay (London: George Allen and Unwin Ltd., 1928). On Benjamin Franklin's odd religious ideas, Kerry S. Walters's *Benjamin Franklin and His Gods* (Urbana, Illinois: University of Illinois Press, 1999) is an entertaining and "enlightening" read.

Chapter 4: Revolutionary Catastrophe

There has been a major revision in the historiography of the French Revolution; it is no longer presented as an unqualified "good thing," and its sinister aspects are becoming much better known than they were a few decades ago. The result is that there are more good books on the Revolution and its main characters than can be listed here, and what follows is a mere sampling.

Simon Schama's *Citizens: A Chronicle of the French Revolution* (New York: Alfred A. Knopf, 1989) is a massive, well-written account of what things were really like in the France of Louis XVI and how the Revolution unfolded. Apt quotations from contemporary sources and telling word pictures of the characters add to its readability.

There are a number of recent books on the counterrevolution in France, most of them scholarly works. Fortunately, Warren H. Carroll's *The Guillotine and the Cross* (Manassas, Virginia: Trinity Communications, 1986) is a thoroughly Catholic account of the Revolution that includes sections on the Vendée rising and other counterrevolutionary activity.

Finally, Dickens's *Tale of Two Cities* should be mentioned as the great English novel about the Revolution, with its unforgettable characters. *The Scarlet Pimpernel*, by the Baroness Orczy is not in the same league as literature, but the 1935 film version with Leslie Howard is well worth seeing.

Note: I have not included any writings of Chesterton or Belloc dealing with the Revolution or its major figures because some things I have read by them give the impression that they actually admired it. In view of the high quality of so much of their other work, I am at a loss to explain this, since the facts about it must have been available in England in their time. Furthermore, while Belloc's numerous biographies make for interesting reading, the complete lack of references makes the historian wary.

On Brother Solomon, see W. J. Battersby, *Brother Solomon, Martyr of the French Revolution* (New York: The Macmillan Company, 1960). The reader gets an insight into the ambiguity of events as seen by those living through them, and the heroism of the many Catholics who died for their Faith.

There is an interesting collection of papers from a Hillsdale College symposium on the French Revolution: *Reflections on the French Revolution: A Hillsdale Symposium*, edited by Stephen Tonsor (Washington, DC: Regnery Gateway, 1990). Some take a rather benign view of the Revolution, and others analyze the role played by of Enlightenment ideas and other topics. I bought it for the essay by Erik Ritter von Kuehnelt-Leddihn, "The Age of the Guillotine," and have not regretted it.

I have found all the works of Dr. von Kuehnelt-Leddihn that I have read extremely worthwhile, although too numerous to list here. One that touches on themes that derive from the French revolutionary slogan, "Liberty, Equality, Fraternity," is *Liberty or Equality—The Challenge of Our Time* (Caldwell, Idaho: The Caxton Printers, Ltd., 1952).

Chapter 5: Napoleon and After

It would take a whole volume to list the biographies of Napoleon and the studies of his military tactics, politics, and government. The man and his career seem to exert an endless fascination on every generation. I am not familiar with any good Catholic appraisal of the emperor. Belloc's lengthy biography has the usual defect of all his works in its lack of citations, which is particularly irritating in the case of the apparently supernatural incident with which the book closes, with its optimism about what seems to be the hero's speedy salvation. On the other hand, there is a fascinating collection of Bonaparte's actual words in *The Mind of Napoleon*, edited and translated by J. Christopher Herold (New York: Columbia University Press, 1955). Included are his thoughts on politics, the

Church ("There are only two powers in the world—the sword and the spirit.... In the long run, the sword is always beaten by the spirit"), law, society, war, and of course, himself. Browsing a collection like this gives us at least partial insight into the thought processes of the little man who made such a big splash in history.

An old biography of Blessed Anna Maria Taigi, *Wife, Mother and Mystic*, by Albert Bessières, S.J. (Rockford, Illinois: TAN Books and Publishers, 1952 [reprint]), leaves much to be desired as a biography but does give a picture of both a saintly soul and the situation of Italy in the Napoleonic era. The book is flawed by the author's preoccupation with the fate of Napoleon's family, but those details have some attraction for those interested in the history of the period. A biography of another saintly Italian involved in the upheaval of the Napoleonic invasions of Italy is Msgr. Leon Cristiani's *A Cross for Napoleon: The Life of Father Bruno Lanteri* (Boston: Daughters of St. Paul, 1981 [reprint]). This is a most interesting account of a little-known priest whose life became entangled in the turmoil of the French conquests.

A World Restored, by Dr. Henry A. Kissinger is not a Catholic book, but it presents a scholarly account of the conservative politics of Metternich and the balanced achievements of the Congress of Vienna, with applications made to the world of the 1950s, when it was written (it has appeared in a number of editions by several publishers since then).

Many writers have explored the intellectual issues brought out by the clashing ideologies of the revolutionary and post-revolutionary era. *Catholic Political Thought 1789–1848*, by Bela Menczer (London: Burnes Oates and Washbourne, Ltd., 1953) has been reprinted at least once by the University of Notre

Dame Press. It is a collection of texts from major Catholic thinkers such as Metternich, Cortés, and de Maistre, some of whom we have met and others who will be mentioned later. Thomas Molnar's *The Counter-Revolution* (New York: Funk and Wagnalls, 1969) is an interesting analysis; many of the authors and others mentioned in the work will be unfamiliar to the general reader, although serious students will find it rewarding.

Fr. Felix Sarda y Salvany's little work, *What Is Liberalism?*, was first published in 1899 and reprinted by TAN Books in 1979. It is sobering in its straightforwardness ("Liberalism is a sin,") timely, and instructive. Some of it is also dated—because the liberalism of today manifests itself differently and more subtly than that of 1899—and in places perhaps overly narrow-minded. Still, it is refreshing to read a work that warns us so forthrightly against the essence of liberal thinking; we can all use the reminder.

Chapter 6: The Mid-Nineteenth Century

There is space for only a few titles dealing with the mid-nineteenth century here, although on every topic briefly mentioned in chapter 6 numerous books have been written. Carlton Hayes's *Political and Social History of Modern Europe*, Volume 2 gives a somewhat outdated but easy-to-follow overview of the period beginning with 1815. Daniel-Rops's *The Church in an Age of Revolution*, Volume 2 is part of his multivolume *History of the Church of Christ*. Some of his later writings are tinged with liberalism, but for the facts of the period his work is valuable. Priscilla Robertson's *Revolutions of 1848: A Social History* (Princeton, New Jersey: Princeton University Press, 1967) is a good survey of the topic, and J. M. Thompson's *Louis Napoleon and the Second Empire* (New York: W. W. Norton & Company,

Inc., 1967) is a readable work by a well-known British historian. Finally, *The Great Hunger*, by Cecil Woodham-Smith (New York: New American Library, 1962) was a best seller when it first appeared in 1962 detailing the then little-known Irish famine.

On Darwin

Many works on evolution and Darwin have come out recently that are not listed here but can be found online, along with online debates on the topic and the popular film *Expelled*. The works below represent only a sample of what's out there.

R. F. Baum, *Doctors of Modernity: Darwin, Marx, and Freud* (Peru, Illinois: Sherwood Sugden and Co., 1988): Interesting material on Darwin's own doubts about the evolution of mind; also good on the defects common to all the "doctors." Very good reading.

The several works by Phillip E. Johnson refuting Darwin and Darwinism from different angles are all worth reading.

Cornelius G. Hunter, *Darwin's God—Evolution and the Problem of Evil* (Grand Rapids, Michigan: Brazos Press, 2001): I think this one is terrific. It dissects Darwin's illogical presuppositions, such as blind chance "selecting" and "designing," and also the constant pseudo argument that "God wouldn't have done things this way."

Michael J. Behe, *Darwin's Black Box* (first published in 1996; various editions since then): A classic refutation of Darwnism by appealing to the molecular evidence.

Michael J. Behe, William A. Dembski, Stephen C. Meyer, *Science and Evidence for Design in the Universe* (San Francisco: Ignatius Press, 2000): This is a collection of papers presented at a Wethersfield Institute conference in 1999.

Suggestions for Further Reading

I still use a handy little TAN publication called *The Evolution Hoax Exposed*, a 1971 reprint of a 1941 work by A. N. Field. Whoever he was, he sure made sense.

On Marx

Charles J. McFadden, O.S.A., *The Philosophy of Communism* (New York: Benziger Brothers, Inc., 1963): Archbishop Sheen called this "Without a doubt, the best treatment of the philosophy of Communism in any language." I used it as a homeschool textbook for high school. It is ingeniously planned so that the first half of the book presents various aspects of Communist doctrine so persuasively that one is almost convinced of some of its arguments. The second half of the book refutes the arguments made. An extremely effective method.

Chapter 7: The Late Nineteenth Century

For the general history of this period, the surveys of Daniel-Rops, Hughes, and Carlton Hayes, referred to in earlier chapters, are useful. A good overview of East Central Europe is *Borderlands of Western Civilization*, by the Polish historian Oscar Halecki (New York: The Ronald Press Company, 1952). There are several recent histories of Hungary in English, but I find an older work of C. A. Macartney, *Hungary: A Short History* (Edinburgh: The University Press, 1962) more readable and generally informative.

Catholic Social and Political Thought

On Msgr. Freppel, Bishop of Angers, there have been several articles in issues of *The Catholic Counter-Reformation in the Twenty-First Century*.

The *Syllabus* of Pope Pius IX, summarizing modern errors on many points, is widely available and should be familiar to all Catholics. A work edited by Anne Freemantle, *The Papal Encyclicals in Their Historical Context*, contains selections from many papal documents. It includes the *Syllabus* as well as a selection from Pope Pius's last encyclical, to the bishops of Prussia, dealing with Bismarck's Kulturkampf. In an introduction to the section on Pius IX, Miss Freemantle includes a telling quotation from Prince Metternich, referring to the pope's liberal leanings, which changed after 1848: "A liberal pope is not a possibility.... He can destroy but he cannot build. What the Pope has already destroyed by his liberalism is his own temporal power; what he is unable to destroy is his spiritual power."

The Saints

For the visions of St. Catherine Labouré, there are a number of accounts. The first full-length life of this saint to be published in the United States, the well-written fruit of years of research, is *Saint Catherine Labouré of the Miraculous Medal*, by Father Joseph I. Dirvin, C.M. (New York: Farrar, Straus and Company, 1958).

Forty Dreams of St. John Bosco, compiled by Fr. J. Bacchiarello, S.D.B., was published in 1969 and reprinted in paperback by TAN Books in 1996.

Fanchón Royer is the author of *St. Anthony Claret: Modern Prophet and Healer* (New York: Farrar, Straus and Cudahy, 1957).

A wonderful German work by Rev. Constantine Kempf, S.J., was published in an English translation in 1916 as *The Holiness of the Church in the Nineteenth Century* (New York: Benziger Brothers). It includes over four hundred pages on saintly men and women of the 1800s; many of those listed as Venerable or Blessed have since been canonized, such as St. John Bosco,

Suggestions for Further Reading

St. Thérèse of Lisieux, St. John Vianney, and St. Elizabeth Seton. The work makes for fascinating and heartening reading.

Chapter 8: The Century of Total War: Part One

Thunder at Twilight: Vienna 1913–1914, by Frederic Morton (New York: Charles Scribner's Sons, 1989) is an extraordinarily evocative sketch of the Austrian capital just before the outbreak of the War. Trotsky, Stalin, and Hitler—all young and obscure figures at the time—were just some of those celebrating the carnival season of 1913 in Vienna. Having set the stage, Morton proceeds to a day-by-day and almost hour-by-hour account of the flurry of telegrams and consultations that went on among the great powers until the final and fatal decisions were made.

Warren Carroll's *1917: Red Banners, White Mantle* (Front Royal, Virginia: Christendom Press, 1981) is a short and gripping account of the Russian Revolution, complete with the creepy figure of Rasputin. The same author's *Rise and Fall of the Communist Revolution* (Front Royal, Virginia: Christendom Press, 1995) goes into more detail on the Russian Revolution as well as the development of the Communist Empire.

On Modernism

Michael Davies's *Partisans of Error—St. Pius X against the Modernists* (Long Prairie, Minnesota: Neumann Press, 1983) is definitely a useful treatment, although brief; the introduction is by Paul Hallett (quoted earlier). For the facts of the controversy, the best general treatment seems to be that of the *Catholic Encyclopedia* available online. Some biographies of St. Pius contain little specific information on Modernism, but are useful for background and the mentality of the great pope: a popularly written life of Pius X is *The Great Mantle*, by Katherine

Burton (New York: Longman, Green and Co., 1950). *Pius X*, by Fr. Hieronymo Dal-Gal (Westminster, Maryland: Newman Press, 1954), is drawn from the accounts of witnesses consulted for the saint's beatification and canonization. There is only one brief mention of Modernism as such, but the book is well worth reading.

On Fatima

As mentioned earlier, the works of Brother Michel and Brother François are by far the most complete accounts of the apparitions. Sister Lucy's several memoirs are also valuable.

Chapter 9: The Century of Total War: Part Two

On the eugenics movement, a good place to go for information about Margaret Sanger and her ilk is the Human Life International Website: http://www.hli.org. On the German euthanasia program, there are many recent works. I use a small book excerpted from Dr. Frederic Wertham's large work, *A Sign for Cain*, entitled *The German Euthanasia Movement* (Cincinnati: Hayes Publishing Company, Inc., 1978). The statistics, quotations, and clear narrative make for gripping reading.

On the spread of Communism, see Warren Carroll's *The Rise and Fall of the Communist Revolution* (Front Royal, Virginia: Christendom Press, 1995); also consult Dr. Carroll's bibliography. A classic, balanced work by a secular historian is Hugh Thomas's 1961 work, *The Spanish Civil War* (numerous editions). For the Soviet Union, see Fr. Walter J. Ciszek's *With God in Russia* (multiple editions).

On the Catholic Church in the war years, numerous works have been written. One large volume dating from 1941, unfortunately anonymously written to protect the author, is a thorough documentation of the persecution of the Church in Germany and includes Pius XI's encyclical on Nazism, the text of the Concordat between Germany and the papacy, and examples of the unrelenting Nazi propaganda against Pope Pius XII. On a clerical hero of Rome during the German occupation, Monsignor O'Flaherty, see J. P. Gallagher's *The Scarlet Pimpernel of the Vatican*, published in 1967 and reprinted a number of times. The movie based on it, *The Scarlet and the Black*, is generally excellent, although it portrays Pope Pius XII (briefly) as rather wimpish. On Walter Duranty and his successful disinformation about the famine in Ukraine, see *Stalin's Apologist*, by S. J. Taylor (New York: Oxford University Press, 1990).

Among the numerous studies of World War II, a fine comprehensive study is *A World at Arms: A Global History of World War II*, by Gerhard L. Weinberg (New York: Cambridge University Press, 1994). Patrick J. Buchanan's *Churchill, Hitler, and the Unnecessary War* (New York: Crown Publishers, 2008) is a brilliant, controversial work that is also an enjoyable read.

Chapter 10: Postwar and Post–Cold War

For the Liberation in France, there are few reliable works in English. One of them is by British journalist Sisley Huddleston, who was an eyewitness: *France: The Tragic Years* (several editions, the first in 1955).

Meeting at Potsdam, by Charles L. Mee, Jr. (New York: M. Evans & Company, Inc., 1975) is an eye-opening and detailed account of the conference that marked the beginning of the Cold War and sealed the fate of Eastern Europe. The bias (or naivety) of the author does not prevent the book from being a readable day-by-day chronicle with numerous interesting quotations from Truman, Churchill, and Stalin.

The Church Under Attack

Many accounts of the Hungarian Revolution exist and cannot all be listed here. A very readable one is James A. Michener's *Bridge at Andau*, published the year after the event.

Josef Pieper's *Leisure: The Basis of Culture*, highly recommended, has been published in a number of editions and formats; the first English translation was made in 1952.

For the postwar Soviet bloc, see *The Rise and Fall of the Communist Revolution*, by Warren Carroll (Front Royal, Virginia: Christendom Press, 1995).

On Cardinal Mindszenty, his own *Memoirs* (various editions) are primary documentation. *Mindszenty the Man*, by Joseph Vecsey as told to Phyllis Schlafly (St. Louis: Cardinal Mindszenty Foundation, 1972) is a readable introduction to the cardinal's story, as is *Cardinal Mindszenty: Confessor and Marty of Our Time*, by József Közi-Horváth (Chichester: Aid to the Church in Need/Augustine Publishing Company, 1979).

For Fatima, *The Whole Truth about Fatima* series mentioned in previous chapters, including the volume to be found as an e-book at http://www.crc-internet.org/, is the most thoroughly researched source.

About the Author

Dr. Diane Moczar is a former professor of history at Northern Virginia Community College. She received a bachelor's degree in history at San Francisco College for Women, and following two years' research in Paris on a Fulbright Grant she obtained a master's degree at Columbia University. Her doctoral work was completed at Catholic University and George Mason University. She has written for *The Latin Mass, National Review, Smithsonian, Catholic Digest,* and many other publications. She is also the author of *Ten Dates Every Catholic Should Know, Islam at the Gates, Converts and Kingdoms,* and *Don't Know Much about Catholic History.*

An Invitation

Reader, the book that you hold in your hands was published by Sophia Institute Press. Sophia Institute seeks to nurture the spiritual, moral, and cultural life of souls and to spread the Gospel of Christ in conformity with the authentic teachings of the Roman Catholic Church.

Our press fulfills this mission by offering translations, reprints, and new publications that afford readers a rich source of the enduring wisdom of mankind.

We also operate two popular online Catholic resources: CrisisMagazine.com and CatholicExchange.com.

Crisis Magazine provides insightful cultural analysis that arms readers with the arguments necessary for navigating the ideological and theological minefields of the day. *Catholic Exchange* provides world news from a Catholic perspective as well as daily devotionals and articles that will help you to grow in holiness and live a life consistent with the teachings of the Church.

In 2013, Sophia Institute launched Sophia Institute for Teachers to renew and rebuild Catholic culture through service to Catholic education. With the goal of nurturing the spiritual, moral, and cultural life of souls, and an abiding respect for the role and work of teachers, we strive to provide materials and programs that are at once enlightening to the mind and ennobling to the heart; faithful and complete, as well as useful and practical.

www.SophiaInstitute.com
www.CatholicExchange.com
www.CrisisMagazine.com
www.SophiaInstituteforTeachers.org